GOD'S MISSION

—————— A N D ——————

POSTMODERN CULTURE

GOD'S MISSION

AND

POSTMODERN CULTURE

THE GIFT OF UNCERTAINTY

John C. Sivalon

ORBIS BOOKS
Maryknoll, New York 10545

Cataloging-in-Publication Data
Sivalon, John C.
    God's mission and postmodern culture : the gift of uncertainty / John C. Sivalon.
        p.   cm.
    Includes index.
    ISBN 978-1-57075-999-4
    1. Missions – Theory. 2. Catholic Church – Missions. 3. Postmodernism – Religious aspects – Christianity. 4. Christianity and culture. I. Title.
BV2180.S58 2012
266'.2 – dc23   2012007069

Contents

Preface

In 2002 I was elected general superior of the Maryknoll Fathers and Brothers. After ten years of having had almost nothing official to do with the hierarchy of the Roman Catholic Church, I was thrust into a daily exchange with the reality and culture of this group.[1] As I related to them over my six-year term, it became clear to me that a dramatic change was taking place in the church that had formed me in my seminary years.

Ordained in 1975, following ten years of training, I was of that generation of seminarians most affected by the energy and vision of the Second Vatican Council. I accepted the changes proposed by Vatican II with enthusiasm and pursued my ministry driven by the hope that eventually I would see the fruition of that new vision of mission and church. Instead, as I related to the church hierarchy more closely, I came to see that many of them portrayed as a misrepresentation the vision of Vatican II to which I had committed myself. In its place, their interpretation seemed to me to propose a return to a church that I had known in the 1950s.

One of the fresh developments of Vatican II was that the Roman Catholic Church, after nearly four hundred years, was finally coming to some recognition of the goodness of the modern world. This was epitomized by Vatican II's Pastoral Constitution on the Church in the Modern World.[2] Developments in science, scientific knowledge, and other disciplines were presented in this document as having a value and integrity in their own right. The document concedes that when understood properly, this knowledge is not contradictory to the Christian faith.

Yet as I listened to church officials and read official pronouncements, it became increasingly obvious that they were characterizing much of Western modern culture as relativistic, secularized, and increasingly non-Christian. I found that their reaction against the more progressive aspects of Vatican II was mirrored in their reaction against the social developments in modern Western culture, which I refer to as "postmodern culture" in this book. As I reacted against their stance toward Vatican II, I also came to realize that I was reacting against the way they related to European and North American postmodern culture.

As a missionary, I taught sociology at the University of Dar es Salaam, which obviously pressed me to take culture seriously in trying to understand people's behavior. Furthermore, joining this perspective to theology led me naturally to a more contextual approach of theological method. In this understanding, the context of the community, including the political, social, economic, and cultural aspects, are extremely important as a source of God's revelation. Contextual theology is based on the belief that God is present in all cultures.

My early experience in a very rural setting in Tanzania only reinforced this perspective. I witnessed firsthand how the Kuria people struggled to understand their faith from the perspective of their own culture. This experience, as I describe in chapter 1, was an impetus for me to take postmodern culture as seriously as I would any other culture in discerning God's will and wisdom.

This book, as I have discovered in writing it, is an attempt to make sense of a tremendously varied life in Christian mission that has led me through a series of questions over the years to finally ask: What is the meaning of Christian mission in this age of postmodern culture? On the one hand, I am deeply committed to the Christian faith that was nourished in me by the Roman Catholic tradition. On the other hand, I believe deeply in the presence of God in all cultures, including our own postmodern culture. In order, then, to adequately respond to the question above concerning the relevance of mission in the twenty-first century, I believe we need to search out the answer by taking seriously our own culture and God's presence in it. We need to listen and discern God's wisdom and will within our postmodern culture.

In the process of preparing this work, I received special institutional support from both Union Theological Seminary as a scholar-in-residence and from the University of Scranton as a visiting professor. I have been aided immensely by a number of friends, colleagues, and professionals. The first two deserving of special mention are the two theologians who have most dramatically impacted my own thought. They are Roger Haight and William Frazier. Besides them, Lee Cormie, who directed my doctoral work, has remained a source of support and inspiration, especially in his commitment to contextual theology and the struggles of the peoples of Latin America, Africa, and Asia. I am especially grateful to Robert Ellsberg for his professional advice as a writer and publisher and to Linda A. Unger, who has edited a number of drafts of this work and engaged in clarifying discussions concerning many of its ideas.

I also bothered a number of people to read drafts of it and to offer their critiques and suggestions. I want to thank my colleagues Dave Schwinghamer, Dave Brown, Joe Healey, Jim Noonan, Dick Baker, and again Roger Haight, who willingly read and commented on an entire earlier draft. Also, a very special acknowledgment must be given to those four missionaries who wrote their own reflections for chapter 5. I am deeply thankful to them not only for what they wrote, but even more, for the inspiration that their lives and visions have been for me. I thank Jim Noonan, Theresa Baldini, Madeline McHugh, the late Doug Venne, and Marty Shea. All of them also read earlier drafts and made significant and very helpful observations. It is their deep sense of the presence of God that I hope I adequately portray in the coming pages: God present in postmodern culture revealing to us a fresh understanding of God's mission and our call to participate in it through a new way of being and doing.

I have sought to employ gender-inclusive language. However, the limits of my own stylistic ability keep me from further reducing the use of masculine pronouns when speaking of the Trinity. It is clear that there are difficulties with the traditional appellation of Father, Son, and Holy Spirit. The use, however, of more inclusive names such as the "Source," the "Wellspring," and the "Living Water," I find, fail to fully convey the depth and intricacy of the mystery of the Trinity, especially in that section of the book dealing with the presentation of von Balthasar's "super-kenosis." I hope these linguistic difficulties will not hinder the reader from seeing past them into the beauty of the mystery we call God.

Introduction

This book is an attempt to show that postmodern culture does not render Christian mission meaningless; quite the contrary, it breathes fresh insight, vision, and life into Vatican II's notion that mission is centered in the very heart of God.

In 1972 I walked into a world that seemed quite unfamiliar and extraordinary. Houses were roofed with thatch; men were walking around with beer straws made of reeds; young men and women were being circumcised shortly after puberty; extended families were celebrating feasts with sacrifices of cattle, dancing, and other religious rituals to mark the entrance of old men into elderhood; and churches were filled with young and old, men and women vibrantly celebrating their faith. In the fall of 2001, I returned home to the United States and found myself in an almost equally peculiar and wondrous culture. People were talking and texting one another almost incessantly yet apparently oblivious to those in their actual physical presence; popular culture appeared outrageous as images of the hyper-real dominated; greed and super-accumulation of wealth seemed normative; the world with its diversity of peoples, cultures, languages, goods, and services was present in the local; and, most astonishingly, churches seemed curiously empty and almost totally devoid of young people.[1] Where had they gone, and how had the church become so marginal to so many?

When I went as a missionary to rural Tanzania, I was originally mentored by a man who by then already had worked as a missionary with the Kuria people for twenty-five years.[2]

This missionary introduced me to their traditions and values and showed me that there was something much deeper and more valuable in their culture than the surface observations I had made. More important, he allowed me to accompany him while he attempted to live a different way of mission.

His way of mission was to discover God in the culture of the people without imposing Western values or customs on them. Against some opposition from other missionaries and some Tanzanians, he looked for the transformative elements within the culture of the Kuria rather than imposing a transformation from without. I vividly recall the celebration of his twenty-fifth anniversary of ordination in the pew-less[3] church in Kei-sangora village. After hearing someone praise him for all his efforts and actually make reference to his "bringing light into the darkness," he strongly clarified that the "light" had been with the Kuria people all along. The "light" was in their culture and not something that he brought.

His vision reinforced my own understanding of "inculturation" as I began my missionary life. In the theology of mission, "inculturation" is a term whose meaning has changed over time. It originally referred to simply translating the scriptures into the vernacular of the people. It then expanded to include adapting particular rituals, church buildings, teachings, and church administrative structures to make them more relevant to the culture and more easily understood by the people. Often it has been used in a distorted fashion interchangeably with "acculturation," which refers mainly to expatriate missionaries adapting to the culture.

In this book, however, "inculturation" is understood in the way expressed by Pope Benedict XVI in *Verbum Domini:*

> The authentic paradigm of inculturation is the incarnation itself of the Word: "acculturation" or

"inculturation" will truly be a reflection of the incarnation of the Word when a culture, transformed and
regenerated by the Gospel, brings forth from its own
living tradition original expressions of Christian life,
celebration and thought.[4]

Inculturation as incarnation,[5] emphasizes that God is
actively revealing God's self in culture. We are charged through
the gift of grace and the Holy Spirit to discover that incarnated
God in all cultures. Just as inculturation leads Christians,
church leaders, and theologians in those areas to read the cultures of Asia, Africa, and Latin America in order to discover the
voice of God, I believe it equally moves us to search out that
voice of God in our own North American and European cultures, and today particularly in what I call postmodern culture.

Like Kuria culture, postmodern culture is characterized by
values and beliefs much deeper than my initial surface observations described above would indicate. These values and
beliefs will be more fully developed in the next chapter, but
they can be quickly summarized as a strong sense of the historical development of ideas and understandings; an unquestioned acceptance of the social construction of knowledge and
the influence of cultures on understanding; and, finally, an
awareness of the immensity, diversity, complexity, and mystery of the social and physical worlds.

Because of these characteristics, postmodern culture has
been rejected almost out of hand by some Roman Catholic
and other Christian church leaders as leading necessarily to
nihilistic relativism. This reaction, I believe, has contributed
to the marginalization of the church from the life of many
people in Europe and North America, especially the young. By
not taking seriously the presence of God in our own culture,
the church relegates itself to becoming an interesting artifact,

while many people search for meaning and nourishment in other spiritual expressions or mixture of expressions.

Equally strong is the reaction of many who are deeply steeped in postmodern culture to reject outright any sense of the value of Christian missionary activity. While they may accept the right of an individual to believe in the Christian narrative, they do not embrace it and find it hard to value taking this narrative to others in a different cultural milieu. They demand a respect for diversity, including religious diversity, which clearly questions the universal character of any religious expressions.

I find myself struggling in a middle space. I firmly believe in the value of the Christian narrative and the need to carry it forward. And I firmly believe that God is incarnate in postmodern culture just as much as God is incarnate in any culture. As such, there is a necessary revelatory aspect to postmodern culture that we must read and respect as we search for a relevant understanding of the mystery of God and of God's Mission.

When I began my missionary career, I believed that Vatican II had set the church on a radically new course and that eventually the ideas of mission and church it developed, or at least implied, would naturally grow. The most significant of these for mission will be explained in chapter 3, but it needs to be at least mentioned here, and that is Missio Dei.

This concept emphasizes that mission is God's Mission. This is a major shift from the idea of mission being something that we do, or something that belongs to the church. I believed that this shift would have major consequences. I looked forward to seeing some radical changes in my lifetime in the ways in which we Christian expatriate missionaries see ourselves; how as a Christian community we relate to others; and how seriously we take our own evolving postmodern culture, which is becoming more global in character.

More recently, though, what appears to have happened is a swing back to a much more conservative interpretation of the Second Vatican Council. In this book, I refer to those leading this shift, mainly but not exclusively bishops, as "romantic conservatives."[6] Their interpretation and emphases appear to me to be based directly on a fear of and reaction against postmodern culture. This can be seen in their demands for uniformity as the sign of unity. This gets expressed most succinctly as "loyalty to the Church is obedience." It is also reflected in their proclaiming Roman Catholic "magisterium" as the fullness of truth without nuance or historical sensitivity. This has become more dramatic as they have gradually extended the role of papal infallibility by including a variety of teachings under a category of "definitive."[7] Finally, they have refocused mission on what they call the "New Evangelization," which is in fact their call for a reevangelization of Europe and North America by creating a renewed "Christian culture" in opposition to postmodern culture.[8]

Over against these restoration ideas,[9] I seek to recover the fervor for change that Vatican II initiated and to further develop its concept of mission through the understanding of revelation given to us by God today in postmodern culture. I seek to do this partially by bringing together my understanding of the theologies of Roger Haight[10] and William Frazier.[11]

As I have struggled to understand my faith and Christian mission, I have been deeply influenced by these two theologians of dramatically different perspectives. Upon their thought, I have tried to build my own negotiated understanding of being deeply committed to Christian mission and open to the revelatory aspect of postmodern culture.

I have studied under both and respect each of them for their academic rigor and, more important, for their commitment and faith. While each would see himself in line with more liberal post–Vatican II presentations, neither of them finds his thought compatible with the other's. However, I find a real resonance between them through their understanding of inculturation as incarnation. Both have recognized the influence of postmodern culture on their thought, Haight emphasizing the reading and discerning of God's wisdom and revelation in this culture for developing a transdenominational ecclesiology, and Frazier finding in the thought of Jacques Derrida a nonbelieving companion for his understanding of the mystery of life through death.

In brief, this book is an attempt to show that postmodern culture does not render Christian mission meaningless; quite the contrary, it breathes fresh insight, vision, and life into Vatican II's notion that mission is centered in the very heart of God. Mission is God's loving embrace of creation, with all that that implies. This embrace is no less real today than it was in 1950 or earlier and it is no less an embrace of postmodern culture than it is of any culture around the world.

Among the revelatory elements of postmodern culture, one that I think is essential for the purposes of this book and that will be developed more fully in chapters 1 and 2 is "Uncertainty." For some, uncertainty denotes ambiguity or confusion and so is seen as a source of anxiety and tension. But what if using the lens of postmodern culture instead, we see uncertainty as a reality that marks the social and physical world and as such, a gift. For one thing, uncertainty is the ground of questioning. It leads the curious to ask: Why we are doing this? What should we do? or How is it best done?

Among expatriate missionaries I think their common experience has pushed them to develop uncertainty as a common character trait.[12] It is a trait that comes from living in a culture that is not their own and that they know they will never fully understand. It comes from speaking a language with childlike proficiency and yet being expected to lead religious ceremonies, teach in schools, and publicly represent a community. It comes from preaching Gospel demands that they are never quite sure fit, and even if they do, how well they are understood. It is this kind of uncertainty that leads to a very real sense of their own humanness and vulnerability that marks so many expatriate missionaries. As such it also opens their eyes and minds to be much more sensitive to the reality of uncertainty fostered within postmodern culture.

In the coming chapters, I hope to show uncertainty to be much more than just this character trait or a ground for questioning. I hope to show that the lens of postmodern culture from a variety of perspectives reveals it to be an integral element of reality that God is offering us as a gift. For the gift of uncertainty portends the gift of faith. The gift of uncertainty initiates the gifts of contemplation and discernment. The gift of uncertainty births the gifts of imagination and creativity. The gift of uncertainty generates the gift of change and growth. And, most important, the gift of uncertainty grounds our mission within the Mission of God. All of these points are the major characteristics and consequences for mission that will be developed in future chapters when the Mission of God ("Missio Dei") is looked at anew from the perspective of God's voice within postmodern culture.

In chapter 1, I more fully develop some of the points that were mentioned in this chapter, including some of the major shifts in thinking that have taken place since Vatican II, and draw a fuller picture of what postmodern culture is. Borrowing hermeneutical and scientific concepts from that culture, I apply them in chapter 2 to understanding the mystery of God as Trinity as the foundation for discerning mission as God's Mission. Within the Christian narrative, most would profess that Jesus is central to revealing who God is, and so, in chapter 3, using the eyes of postmodern culture, I challenge us to look beyond the taken-for-granted understandings of the death and resurrection of Jesus and use those mysteries to more deeply delve into the heart of God, of whose Mission we speak. In chapter 4 I use the very traditional elements of integral evangelization to more explicitly highlight how God's Mission viewed through the values of postmodern culture leads to radical shifts in how we understand proclamation, witness, dialogue, worship, and human development. These shifts will be further highlighted in chapter 5 by looking at the lived expressions of this renewed sense of God's Mission as four different groups of missionaries describe their lives in Guatemala, Sudan, Bangladesh, and Cambodia. Finally, in chapter 6, I hope to bring together the insights of those lived experiences with my own perceptions of God's Mission as revealed in postmodern culture. I do this knowing that those church leaders and faithful who reject postmodern culture out of hand will probably not be convinced. Nor do I think that those who reject out of hand any value to Christian missionary activity will be persuaded by my arguments. I do hope, though, that those who find themselves, like me, struggling in that middle space, trying to make sense of their Christian faith within the culture in which we live, will find some amount of accompaniment in this work. We are called to go forward then by taking seriously our faith, that God is alive and incarnated in all cultures, and this includes what I have labeled here postmodern culture.

1

Questioning the Legitimacy of Mission

Beginning in 1965, when I first expressed an interest in becoming a Roman Catholic expatriate missionary, a number of events have occurred both in the world and in the church that have produced widespread skepticism about the whole missionary enterprise.

A small group of Roman Catholic missionaries, their relatives, and some friends were sitting in a New York living room, chatting over drinks. "I really don't care what another person believes as long as they don't try to force their beliefs on me," voiced a middle-aged woman. Immediately, a missionary turned to me and said, "Now, there's your postmodern attitude!" He knew well my interest in trying to understand our role as expatriate missionaries in a cultural field permeated with attitudes that some describe as "postmodern." Whether the woman's remark that evening really can be characterized as postmodern is debatable.[1] Nonetheless, it does reflect the seismic fissure that has occurred between a pre–Vatican II Roman Catholic understanding of Christian mission and the view held by many active Roman Catholics, including missionaries in the United States and Western Europe.

Imagine Pope Benedict XVI sitting in that living room and hearing an active Roman Catholic proclaim that she "doesn't care" what another person believes as long as that person doesn't try to force those beliefs on her. Among other documents, he would likely refer her to *Dominus Iesus*, the declaration that the Congregation for the Doctrine of the Faith under his leadership issued in the year 2000 to correct, what they called, errant understandings about pluralism:

> [The Church] . . . must be primarily committed to proclaiming to all people the truth definitively revealed by the Lord, and to announcing the necessity of conversion to Jesus Christ and of adherence to the Church through Baptism and the other sacraments, in order to participate fully in communion with God, the Father, Son, and Holy Spirit.[2]

Some of the missionaries sitting in that room may have subscribed to *Dominus Iesus*, though they didn't say so. Certainly, most Roman Catholic expatriate missionaries before Vatican II would have gone overseas with that understanding. They were highly motivated by a self concept that was based on the belief that "outside the Church there is no salvation."[3] For them, the salvation of every person in the world depended upon their not only hearing the Gospel but having the opportunity to be baptized into a believing community that lived the Roman Catholic faith.

This gave rise to a tremendous fervor for overseas mission. Missionaries sought to establish the church around the world—founding parishes, erecting dioceses, and developing national structures. They built networks of churches, schools, and clinics even in the most remote of places. By the 1960s, it could be said that the church had been established virtually everywhere.

However, beginning in 1965, when I first expressed an interest in becoming a Roman Catholic expatriate missionary, a number of events have occurred both in the world and in the church that have produced widespread skepticism about a *Dominus Iesus* type of understanding of mission and the whole missionary enterprise.[4] The major ones include: watershed changes in the political landscape of countries in Asia, Latin America, and Africa; academic developments in the social sciences, especially sociology and anthropology; dramatic changes in the Roman Catholic Church itself through Vatican II; and the emergence of postmodern culture. It is the final one that some Roman Catholic officials most recently have targeted as a major obstacle to Christian mission. In response they have called for a "New Evangelization" or reevangelization of Europe and North America.[5]

I would like to briefly highlight the first three of these major shifts before moving on to the main material of postmodern culture and Christian mission. Each of these shifts contributed to the development of questions about mission that emerged on an experiential level in my life and in the lives of many other missionaries.

POLITICAL CHANGE

First, the period that extends from the late 1950s to the early 1970s was one in which former colonies in Africa became independent states. As independence movements progressed, the role of the church in Western colonial expansion came under increased fire. Missionaries were often identified with political and economic colonizers, even though frequently they themselves felt much more identified with the people. However, their skin color, culture, language, customs, and worldview tended to mark them as very similar to the expatriate colonials, no matter how they struggled to distance themselves.

Therefore, in many of the newly independent states, a general critique of Western culture accompanied independence, including a critique of Christianity as a foreign religion.

Tanzania gained its independence in 1962. As a young missionary living in newly independent Tanzania, I met many older missionaries who after independence remarked on the difficult and uncomfortable place in which they found themselves, as political forces and ideology criticized the role they had played during decades of colonization. This was cushioned in Tanzania by the presence of President Julius Nyerere and his close relationship to a number of Roman Catholic officials both foreign and local.[6] However, even he was critical of those missionaries who isolated themselves from the struggles of the people and the implementation of Ujamaa (the democratic socialist policies developed by Nyerere and followed by Tanzania from 1967 to 1985), especially by their economic lifestyles.

Unlike Nyerere, there were many less nuanced critiques of missionaries and Christianity by local party cadres who were obviously being influenced by upper-level party ideologues. This included a number of "campaigns" often led by the youth league of the Party. One such campaign targeted Western dress and while it started with miniskirts quickly extended to bell bottom pants for men and other forms of Western clothing of the 1970s seen as an affront to the national culture.

More surprising was the academic emphasis on the role of Christianity during the colonial period without any equal reference to the role of Islam during the period of slavery. In fact, many Roman Catholic missionaries in Tanzania were from Ireland or of Irish extraction, which hardly led them to be overly supportive of the British colonial regime. In fact, their contribution to the peaceful transition to independence has been documented and described, not only in my "Roman Catholicism and the Defining of Tanzanian Socialism from 1953 to 1985," but in a number of other works.[7] Yet, even with that, there still existed among certain forces in Tanzania and sub-Saharan Africa this general critique of Christianity and Christian missionary activity being in bed with colonialism. It stemmed in part from colonial thought like that of David Livingstone's three "Cs" of colonialism that explicitly tied together commerce, Christianity, and civilization.[8]

At the same time these newly independent nations, including Tanzania, were bubbling with excitement and enthusiasm for the future. Many expatriate missionaries like me went to these countries with an equal amount of excitement and enthusiasm for the future. In this early period of independence, the optimism was infectious. The Roman Catholic Church was changing, exemplified by a hierarchy that was becoming more and more indigenous. African culture was increasingly growing in the respect with which it was taken by Christian theologians and church officials. Visible attempts to adjust itself to the new reality made it look like the church was opening up, growing and becoming increasingly relevant.[9] Yet questions remained about the role of expatriate missionaries in the now self-governing and self-sustaining churches.

ACADEMIC CHANGES

Likewise, the social sciences, especially cultural anthropology and sociology, contributed to changing people's thinking about the world and how they perceived other people's cultures during this period. Originally, these disciplines were marked by an evolutionary understanding that employed such concepts as "primitive," "developed," and "civilization," with Western society as the sole reference point.[10] As a result, many early studies in these disciplines were marked by a clear ethnocentrism, in which African, Asian, Latin American, and other customs were presented and judged by Western standards as less developed.[11]

On the basis of challenges from the newly independent people and how they perceived these disciplines and the conclusions of their studies, it became clear to social scientists that their studies needed to be developed much more from within the context of the people themselves. While anthropology had previously concentrated on small rural units that were presented as isolated and untouched by the forces of capitalism, it began to take seriously the lived reality of people and the dynamic qualities of all cultures. Change was now seen as taking place but not in a unilineal evolutionary fashion but rather as the result of the dynamic interchange of differing cultures, economies, and polities. Cultures came to be seen as different and dynamic, but not better or worse, developed or less developed, civilized or primitive.

This critique of ethnocentrism permeated not just the disciplines mentioned above but also began to enter into the commonsense wisdom of people and more specifically the world of expatriate missionaries and their own self-understanding.[12] Major questions about their role in fostering their religious understanding on other peoples led to a period in which some missiologists (theologians dedicated to the study of mission in all its aspects) even called for a temporary moratorium on sending missionaries overseas.[13] Those who remained in the field had to ask themselves, "If there is truth in this ethnocentric critique, then how do we understand the Truth? How do we understand the relevance of the incarnation and the paschal mystery of Jesus for all of humanity?" As we will see later, the depth of this question was greatly expanded by the critique of postmodern culture.

VATICAN II

As dramatic as these political and academic changes were, they in no way compared to the seismic change in the theological self-understanding of Roman Catholic missionaries that occurred because of Vatican II. At Vatican II, the theology of mission underwent a major transformation.[14] The church by its very nature was seen as missionary. This basic shift from the extension of the church into the "missions," to the church as missionary everywhere and foundationally, led to the development of several new perspectives on mission. Vatican II vividly presented the church in new images, like the "People of God" and the "Church as the Sacrament of Universal Salvation," which also led to dramatically new emphases in understanding mission and the way of doing mission.

As I said earlier, in the period preceding Vatican II, the dominant understanding of the church almost identified it with the "Kingdom of God." Because of that, salvation was seen as the product of baptism, being a member of the church, and fidelity to church teaching. Vatican II's reemphasis of the church as the People of God and the Sacrament of Salvation led to an emphasis on the "Kingdom of God" or "Reign of God" as being a broader arena encompassing all of God's activity in all of creation.[15]

Sacrament points to and partially actualizes a bigger reality than itself. Church as sacrament of universal salvation meant that the role of the church was to witness to and serve a broader reality, namely, the Reign of God. Because of this new emphasis, Roman Catholic missionaries began to define themselves and their functions much more broadly. Not only did it mean seeing themselves serving both Catholics and non-Catholics but also determining how that service was defined. While it continued to include church-related religious and sacramental service, a newfound emphasis was placed on community and social development programs and ministries related to justice and peace for all.[16] It also influenced how we perceived our relationship to other religions and other expressions of the Christian faith.

Finally, and this is important for understanding the main topic of this book, Vatican II also reflected the Roman Catholic Church's protracted negotiations and compromise with modernity as a worldview as explained in the next section. This is important because even as the church moved to make this compromise, the world had already moved far beyond modernity to a culture of postmodernity.

POSTMODERN CULTURE

Rooted in the Enlightenment period, modernity prevailed as a paradigm in the West until the early twentieth century.[17] Enlightenment thinkers looked at two earlier strands of philosophy, rational philosophy and empirical philosophy, and attempted to bring them together. Reason came to be seen as an energy brought to observation to yield truth. It is neither a body of innate ideas nor a slave to simple data, revealed knowledge, or authority. Reason and sensate observation were seen as the cornerstones for knowledge of reality.

Based on this, Enlightenment thinkers embraced three principal ideas that fairly well define the spirit of modernity. First of all, they believed in the perfectibility of humanity by humanity. No longer was perfectibility associated only with

God. Rather, it became more and more accepted that humanity's present conditions did not have to be the way they were and that human beings themselves could change those conditions.

Second, Enlightenment thinkers believed that just as the laws of natural movement reside in nature, so must the laws of social movement reside in social reality. No longer was destiny controlled by God or spirits, they believed, but by laws that reside in natural and social life.

Third, philosophy transformed itself into a discipline dedicated to the social critique of existing institutions and the science that would lead to human perfection.[18] It posited that human reason is capable of knowing the inner workings of reality and thus can manipulate and control reality for human purposes. In this way, modern science believed it had hijacked religion's rational and explanatory role. The physical and social sciences gave human beings certainty in terms of how the world worked. Religion, if it had any purpose at all, was reduced to an individualistic, affective role.

After struggling with modernity and the effects of the enlightenment for nearly four hundred years,[19] Vatican II, in its Pastoral Constitution of the Church in the Modern World, expressed the Roman Catholic Church's compromise most succinctly:

> If by the autonomy of earthly affairs we mean that created things and societies themselves enjoy their own laws and values which must be gradually deciphered, put to use, and regulated by men, then it is entirely right to demand that autonomy. Such is not merely required by modern man, but harmonizes also with the will of the Creator. For by the very circumstance of their having been created, all things are endowed with their own stability, truth,

goodness, proper laws and order. Man must respect these as he isolates them by the appropriate methods of the individual sciences or arts. Therefore if methodical investigation within every branch of learning is carried out in a genuinely scientific manner and in accord with moral norms, it never truly conflicts with faith, for earthly matters and the concerns of faith derive from the same God.[20]

However, while the church was proposing this acknowledgement of modernity, the seed of radical change had already been planted within modernity itself and had begun to grow.

Postmodernity is an important later development of the Enlightenment paradigm. A number of people have talked about its origins as far back as the middle nineteenth century. Gerard Mannion, for example, says:

For some, Nietzsche was both its prophet and its chief intellectual midwife. It is marked by the increasing disillusionment with all overarching explanatory hypotheses for the world in general and human beings and societies in particular. Thus "grand narratives" such as religion, political ideologies and even science itself are no longer seen to have "all the answers" to humanity's questions. The postmodern era is thus marked by a shift from belief in certainties and truth claims to more localized and piecemeal factors. The individual is seen as creating his or her own meaning to a certain extent rather than receiving it from without.[21]

Thus, postmodernity is a historical era marked by a culture with clear values and attitudes that influence how people think and act. These attitudes and values have been assimilated into our consciousness over time from developments in philosophy, science, and hermeneutics. This explains some of the confusion concerning the meaning of postmodernity. In future chapters you will see that at times I am referencing science and other times concepts from hermeneutics. All of these developments I believe have articulated into a culture. As a culture it articulates with other cultures and subcultures around the world with varying degrees of influence or dominance over particular individuals.

Postmodernity as a culture may be much more dominant in North America and Europe than it is in other parts of the world or among new immigrant communities in Western countries. Nevertheless, it has entered into the cultural field of peoples in most of the world, generating varying degrees of reaction, resistance, accommodation, or adaptation. Thus we can see that postmodernity is important as a culture, while at the same time recognizing that its influence is mediated through different previously existing cultures and subcultures, rendering a dynamic and exciting picture of the complexity of the issue.

Roger Haight describes the culture of postmodernity with the following features:

> (1) A historical consciousness that is deeper and more radical than that of Modernity; (2) An appreciation of pluralism that is suspicious of all absolute or universal claims; (3) A consciousness of the social construction of self that has completely undermined the transcendental ego of Modernity and encouraged a grasping individualism; (4) A sense of the size, age, complexity and mystery of reality that modern science never even suspected.[22]

In other words, a growing number of people have come to see how once unquestioned worldviews and paradigms have been proven wrong. The earth was once accepted as flat. We now perceive it as actually more oval. We once thought that the universe circled around the earth. Then we learned that the earth isn't even the center of our own galaxy, let alone of the universe. We thought the universe would begin to contract but now see it as potentially expanding forever. Because of this historical consciousness of our knowledge, a very real skepticism has come to permeate how we look upon truth claims and knowledge itself.

Likewise, as Haight claims, we have come to accept not only that human beings are formed by socialization but that all reality is socially constructed. As our understanding of microgenetics and brain science becomes more sophisticated, it becomes clearer that human behavior and human consciousness, including religious belief and unbelief, are jointly formed if not determined by nature and nurture. Thus, very real questions about personal responsibility and freedom are raised within postmodern culture.

Postmodern culture is further characterized by a sense of pluralism in which the only acceptable metanarrative is that there is no possibility of a metanarrative that can explain all things for all time. Nothing is absolute or set in stone, and everything depends on one's particular frame of reference. These principles were reinforced and moved to a much deeper level by developments in the physical sciences that began to emerge in the early twentieth century.

Quantum mechanics and particle physics have made clear at least two propositions that have reinforced a culture of acceptable pluralism and healthy skepticism of meta-narratives. First, a certain level of randomness exists in which subatomic particles act differently than our common perception of medium-sized simple objects like golf balls. Second, the observer effect at the subatomic level directly influences motion, so we can never really know how the particles move when they are not being observed. "Determining the momentum of an electron forbids our designation of its position and vice-versa."[23] Thus, according to this "principle of indeterminacy," certainty is limited to at best statements of probability and not statements of absolute truth.

In terms of the social world, chaos theory is another contributor to the demise of modern science's sense of certainty. It says that in highly volatile systems, which are characterized as highly organized, energetic, and subject to constant change, any disturbance will set off a process of self-reorganization as the system seeks equilibrium. Order eventually emerges, but usually the shape that order ultimately takes and the fluctuation that brings it about are unpredictable.

Revolutions occur in the social world and in individual lives, but we are hardly able to predict how order will emerge and what shape it will take. Social systems are complex, dynamic, and nonlinear and, therefore, unpredictable, random, and remarkably creative. Contrary to the tenets of modernity, chaos theory tells us, it is not possible for us to identify social or natural laws but only to read the patterns that emerge and to remain open to novelty and unpredictability. This theory has led us to the assumption that not only is understanding biased by perspective but, more importantly, absolute truth is impossible because the social world is so complex that we can never wholly grasp it, and, also, at its deepest levels it displays randomness, which makes it simply unpredictable.

SUMMARY

In summary, postmodern culture is made up of a radical historical consciousness that tends to make all truth claims relative. It is open to plural understandings and emphasizes the social construction of all reality. Scientific developments in understanding the complexity of the universe and its immensity raise major questions concerning our ability to know anything with certainty.[24]

A common initial reaction to postmodern culture is to assume its characteristics have negative implications for Christian faith and Christian mission. With all its talk about the impossibility of truth claims and metanarratives, its emphasis on relativity, and its implicit stoic-nihilistic tendencies, postmodern culture is seen quite naturally to question at a foundational level the possibility of revelation, faith, evangelization, and faith-based ethics and morals. This is the context that explains the reaction mentioned above by Roman Catholic officials who issued the *Dominus Iesus* document. They see this culture and the changes it is bringing about as a threat.

When change occurs a number of types of reaction are possible. One is resistance, with a hearkening back to an earlier period that is romanticized or idealized. I believe that *Dominus Iesus* and other recent pronouncements of the Vatican and Roman Catholic Church officials against pluralism and relativism are forms of this romantic conservatism.

Over against this romantic conservatism, I propose that postmodern culture, in questioning modernity's claims of certainty, opens up rather than shuts down the possibility of faith and of a new and exciting understanding of Christian mission. If we scrutinize postmodern culture from the perspective of the "glass half-full" rather than "half-empty," we discover that its questioning of certainty, its interpretive categories, and its scientific understanding of the universe all open up for us the possibility of moving our understanding of Christian mission beyond the borders of the past fifty years since Vatican II.

In all of this, I aim to show that Christian mission in a cultural field permeated by the values of postmodern culture is possible. Not only that, it is possible with fervor and a motivation equal to that which the romantic conservatives propose. I believe the developments of postmodern science, philosophy, and social sciences contain concepts and understandings that have as yet unfathomed richness for the understanding of our God, our faith, and our mission.

The sciences, both physical and social, in the postmodern period have all identified unpredictability, randomness, and openness in the worlds with which they deal. "This unknowable future puts our human projects at great risk," says D. Brian Austin, "so any courageous engagement of that future requires faith, a commitment to things hoped for but not seen."[25]

Consider the wondrous mystery of it all. Everything in the universe is made up of the same basic stuff and in the process of unpredictable change and movement becomes dust or human life. As Austin says,

> Then I fixed my gaze downward (from the Great Smoky Mountains) to a scene much closer but even further away, focusing on the haphazard pile of muddy shoes hastily abandoned at the doorstep a short time ago. The mud, still glistening with the mist that makes dust come to life, harbors mysteries as magnificent as the mountain itself. From that mud, from its carbon, nitrogen, hydrogen, oxygen and assorted metals, a child can be woven. The atoms in that mud, the same kinds of atoms that

comprise children, you and me, have existed for billions of years. Some of them, in all likelihood, at one time were part of a person.[26]

The beauty of creation is that all is dust, and the tremendous variety of things of which we only have a glimpse has been formed through the unpredictable, chaotic transformations and restructuring of mud that involves destruction, annihilation, or extinction that leads to new life. This marvelous, mysterious, random, unpredictable, and ever expanding cosmos in which we reside gives birth to the gift of uncertainty. This gift of uncertainty opens the door, at the very least, to the possibility of faith and hope in an infinite, and according to the Christian narrative, a self-emptying God who is both God of the "dust" and God of the "process," i.e., Mission.

2

Rediscovering Mission
in God

Postmodern culture . . . offers scientific and hermeneutical concepts that analogously help to rejuvenate traditional concepts of Trinity and the Trinity's Mission.

The seeds of postmodernity planted in philosophy, science, and interpretive studies gradually grew into a postmodern cultural milieu in the last century. It can be assumed that the influence of this culture began to be felt by other fields, including theology. Thus, when in the middle of the twentieth century, the concept of mission as Missio Dei[1] (Mission of God) emerged as a major shift in mission theology it reflected, consciously or unconsciously, Christian theologians' attempts to respond to those postmodern forces around them.

Rather than seeing ourselves and the church as having a mission, Missio Dei presents mission as God's dynamic "process" in which we as church are invited to participate. This posture is dramatically different from mission as the propagation of truths and doctrines deemed orthodox for all and for all time.

Vatican II officially supported this shift in its Decree on the Missionary Activity of the Church (*Ad Gentes*) when it said:

> The pilgrim Church is missionary by her very nature, since it is from the mission of the Son and the

> mission of the Holy Spirit that she draws her origin,
> in accordance with the decree of God the Father.[2]

Even though in its development Missio Dei has faded, as explained in endnote 1 of this chapter, it is key to a postmodern theology of mission.[3] To understand Missio Dei, it is absolutely necessary to start with trying to understand God who is believed by most Christians to be a mystery described as Trinity.[4] Who God is and how we understand God determines to a great extent our understanding of the Mission of God. And it is the rejuvenation of this perspective that is key for mission in a postmodern culture.

Postmodern culture is not only a cultural context to which we must respond or react. Like any other culture it contains elements of revelation that are helpful and important for the further development of a theology of Christian mission. While modernity stifled the development of an understanding of God as Trinity, I believe that postmodern culture, while raising some very real questions about religion, at the same time offers scientific and hermeneutical concepts that analogously[5] help to rejuvenate the mystery of the Trinity and the Trinity's Mission for a cultural field permeated with postmodern values.[6]

FIRST ANALOGY:
TRINITY AS A PARADIGM SHIFT

The first analogy relates to how we can speak about the Trinity at all. For those of us who have been born into the Christian faith, many extremely mysterious beliefs seem almost commonplace. We hear that Jesus was divine and human so many times that it just goes in one ear and out the other without any great effect. We hear that God is one and yet three and go on with our lives. Recently, though, a young man was ordained a missionary priest after having converted from Sikhism. He was asked, What was the hardest Christian belief to accept? His reply was the divinity of Jesus and thus the Trinity. He said that it is easy to believe that Jesus was an exemplary human being, a prophet, or a very holy person, but to believe that he is God is a whole different acclamation. This young priest is not alone for, if we take the Trinity seriously, it demands of all of us a total paradigm shift in how we understand God.

By analogy, it is no less dramatic a shift than the revolution of scientific thought that took place in the transition from classical modern physics to postmodern quantum mechanics. Moreover, the process by which this shift took place and continues to take place is very similar.

For example, in science, one can see a physicist looking wonderingly at some anomaly that doesn't fit into previous models. She ponders, she questions, she painstakingly calculates, but it just doesn't work. Then she moves to saying maybe that previous model isn't right or is only partially right. Once she reaches that point, it is only through imagination that she can see her way through to modeling in a radically new way the "hidden but real world of forces and fields."[7] Imagination is that gift of genius that allows one to see in the chaos, the anomalies, and the creative complexity the hidden but real patterns and relationships. And imagination gains its freedom to create when the predominant paradigm has lost its hold.

The Christian community over time has gone through the very same process of having its dominant paradigm shattered by anomalies and then through grace and imagination moving to a radically new image of God. Picture those first disciples of Jesus. They were ardent monotheists who began following Jesus without questioning their dominant paradigm for understanding God. While studying with Jesus a number of questions arose about him and about his message. Some saw him as an itinerant teacher, some as a political savior, and some as an apocalyptic prophet. No one, though, thought he was God. Then with his death, they were thrown into turmoil as all of their presuppositions were questioned and they hid themselves in a room. Then he reappeared with the wounds of his crucifixion.

With their presuppositions removed, they were able to begin to look anew at what he had said and done. They began to imagine differently the mysterious revelation that was given them. On the one hand they recalled how Jesus like other Jewish teachers had referred to there being only one God, but he called that God *Abba*. This use of *Abba* indicated a very special relationship of God the Father to Jesus. Then in Acts 2:36 it is written, "Therefore let the whole house of Israel know beyond any doubt that God has made both Lord and Messiah this Jesus whom you crucified."

John's Gospel reflects a further development in the identification of Jesus with God. This is evident in the prologue, and it becomes more explicit when Jesus himself is quoted as saying, "I and the Father are one" (John 10:30).

References like these are equally available concerning the Holy Spirit. The most profound of them occurs when Jesus breathes the Spirit upon the disciples and says, "As the Father has sent me, so I send you. Receive the Holy Spirit" (John 20:19, 21). These then were the words and events the disciples came to use to describe in the scriptures their reimaged understanding of God.

What followed were centuries of communal imagination, reading the scriptures and looking for the hidden but real patterns of God's revelation. As Paul Collins states,

> The words, formulas and concepts used to express the understanding that God is three yet one are always going to be used in an attempt to bring to expression something which is not only a logical impossibility but also a mystery beyond the competency of human language. The Council of Constantinople in 382 declared that the Godhead should be understood in the following terms: one substance, three "persons," *mia ousia, tres hypostaseis.* This is the technical language of Nicene orthodoxy, which has been received and sometimes restated over the past sixteen centuries.[8]

At different times, the community judged some understandings of the Trinity to be in error. This judgment was made because the understandings did not accurately represent the Trinity in Unity or Unity in Trinity. Monarchianism or adoptionism proposed that Jesus became Christ at his baptism and was adopted by the Father after his death. Sabellianism or modalism stressed that the one God reveals Godself in three different ways or activities in the world. Arianism, or subordinationism, de-accentuated the divinity of Christ and a semi-Arianism talked of Christ as being similar in essence to the Father but subordinate to God the Father. Macedonianism or Pneumatomachi claimed that the Holy Spirit was a created being. All of these are important, for they remind us how easy it is to fall back to a previous paradigm of God rather than continuing to develop this radical new paradigm of the Trinity.

The crux of the matter, then, is how to understand the unity of the three persons of the Trinity as co-eternal, co-equal, and yet distinct, and how to understand each of those persons as fully God, not just in terms of activity but in being, yet they are not three gods but one. Furthermore, how do we hold to the three as coeternal and coequal and yet believe that one proceeds from the other: the Father begets the Son, and the Father with the Son or through the Son breathes the Holy Spirit?

Because it all appears so illogical, modernity seemed to lead believers to set the Trinity aside. Paul Collins stresses this point when he says, "The perception that the concept of the Trinity is merely speculative and possibly a distraction, has shaped the landscape of theological discourse in the West for the past four centuries, at least."[9] Under the forces of modernity it is just easier to speak of one God. With a modernity understanding of reality, to speak of the Trinity almost necessarily leads us to fall into one of the above mentioned errors.

Likewise regarding the Trinitarian mission, one reason for not taking seriously Missio Dei may be the radical nature of the shift that is required when we renew our belief that mission is God's and the accompanying fear of uncertainty. If, for four hundred years, we have been living under a paradigm that understands mission as ours and has engendered a certainty about who we are as missionaries, the displacement of this paradigm will be no less difficult than the struggle of scientists to give up assumed presuppositions of their theories for understanding the mysteries of the universe.

However, with the postmodern enhancing of the paradigm of modernity,[10] the presuppositions of rational certainty, distinct categories, and unchanging laws have been displaced. This has freed our imaginations to consider anew this beautiful mystery from the perspective of postmodern concepts, which show us that the mystery of the Trinity may not be as unique or illogical as modernity would have us think.

SECOND ANALOGY:
TRINITY AS "RELATIONALITY"

Borrowing from David Cunningham's work on the Trinity,[11] I believe that the concepts of "relationality," "differe(a)nce," and "rhetoric" of postmodern hermeneutics plus developments in postmodern science help us understand afresh the great mystery as stated above. How do we understand the unity of the three persons of the Trinity as co-eternal, co-equal, and yet distinct, and how do we understand each of those persons as fully God, not just in terms of their activity but in terms of their being? Yet, they are not three gods but One.

As Cunningham says, one of modernity's characteristics is to categorize elements into discrete units and then to relate these categories in a linear and often hierarchical fashion. One of its implications has been that in modern culture, I, as a person, am told from birth that I am an individual and my development depends upon my individual talents and effort; I am a unique and distinct person. Unfortunately, these commonplace modern perceptions have seeped into our understanding of the Trinity, so that when we talk of the "persons" of the Trinity we tend to think of them as we do of ourselves in the culture of modernity, as unique and distinct individuals with particular roles that are arranged hierarchically.

This has led to a common misrepresentation of the Trinity in which the first person creates and, after sending the Word to redeem, retires to the background to wait in judgment. The Word made flesh dies and is raised and, after breathing

Wisdom to sustain humanity, retires to the background. In this presentation, it is the Spirit that today represents God's presence in the world, while the other two persons are now fairly irrelevant to present-day divine activity. Likewise, according to this misperception, creation, redemption, and sanctification are distinct activities. The first person creates, and creation is done. The second person redeems, and redemption is done. Sanctification, or fulfillment, is the form divine activity takes in our present. All of this contradicts the ancient claim of God as an undivided unity.[12] The claim, in other words, that all that God does is done by God.

In contrast to modernity's drive to divide and categorize everything into distinct, hierarchical, and unidirectional relationships, for postmodern science the borders that separate elements of reality are much fuzzier, as is the possibility of understanding any one element of reality isolated from others. As Austin writes:

> The disciplines of physics and philosophy of science are now quite confident that quantum mechanics has revealed a world radically different from the one pictured by classical concepts. . . . This is not an easy task, since we are being forced to reconsider some extremely well-established notions of what constitutes reality. Among other things, it seems we must abandon what was a bedrock presumption that any physically real object must be subject to causal laws and thus causal explanations, has specific properties regardless of our take on them, and can be located unambiguously in space and time.[13]

Austin is making reference here to several phenomena that have a bearing on how we understand "relationality."

In quantum mechanics, relationship is not just mutual and reciprocal between various particles. Rather there is a depth of oneness or unity that defines relationship in this postmodern science. For example, first, this can be seen in the relationship of the observer to phenomena leading to the principle of indeterminacy. Second, it can be seen in the unity expressed in wave-particle duality. Finally, it is most mysteriously exemplified in the relationship expressed as quantum entanglement.

While it appears to be mysterious and illogical to the modern mind to speak of "one substance and multiple persons," the postmodern mind has no difficulty talking about a substance that exhibits dual characteristics without being either. The theory of unity of subatomic elements called wave-particle duality says that these elements are neither particles nor waves but, rather, exhibit properties of one or the other (without being either) based on the way they are observed.

> Investigations on the nature of light showed that, depending on the kind of experiment performed, light must be described by electromagnetic waves or by particles. Thus the wave aspect appears in the context of diffraction and interference phenomena, whereas the particulate aspect shows up most distinctly in the photoelectric effect.[14]

Therefore, a subatomic element observed in a particular way and in a particular context exhibits properties of a wave sometimes and a particle at others. While not identical, at least analogously, we can see the relevance of this unity in duality for understanding not only the divinity and humanity of Jesus but the personhood of the three-in-one substance.

The intimate relationship of the observer to the observed is another reflection of the depth of unity expressed by a

postmodern concept of "relationality." Even in modern science, especially the social sciences, an observer effect is talked
about. However, the postmodern understanding of observer
effect is radically different from modernity's understanding. The observer effect in modern science was limited to the
observer's perception of reality being affected by the observer's
attitudes, values, and biases. It was limited to subjectivity. In
quantum mechanics the observer effect is a much more radical, active, and objective effect on the observed. It says that the
observed is changed by the act of observation. The principle
of indeterminacy is basically saying that we can never know
reality as it is because the act of observation changes reality
so that the "relationality" of the observer and the observed
become almost one. This highlights analogously the mystery
of indwelling of the persons by one another. As Jesus said, "The
Father and I are one" (John 10:30) and "Whoever has seen me
has seen the Father" (John 14:9). They are so intimately related
They are One.

The idea of indwelling (or perichoresis) and "relationality"
as unity is further supported by postmodern science in the
notion of quantum entanglement:

> It [entanglement] brings to mind a kitten tied up in
> an unraveled ball of wool or the complex personal
> relationship between two human beings. In physics
> though, it refers to a very specific and strange con-
> cept, an idea so bizarre, so fundamental, and so far
> reaching that I have called it the God Effect. Once
> two particles become entangled, it doesn't matter
> where those particles are; they retain an immediate
> and powerful connection that can be harnessed to
> perform seemingly impossible tasks.... At this quan-
> tum level, it is possible to link particles together so

completely that the linked objects become, to all intents and purposes, part of the same thing. Even if these entangled particles are then separated to opposite sides of the universe, they retain this strange connection. Make a change to one particle and that change is instantly reflected in the other(s) however far apart they may be.[15]

Imagine two or more particles linked together so that one can no longer be adequately described without full mention of its counterpart even when light-years apart. They have become so entangled with one another that they continue to be correlated to one another in their behavior as if they were one object. Just so, the Word made flesh is distinct from the Father and yet one with the Father; the Holy Spirit is breathed by the Father through the Son and yet is one with the Father and the Son.[16]

In summary, quantum mechanics describes the relationship of particles to one another as much more than simply mutual and reciprocal. According to them, the observer relates to an observed element and in doing so, changes the element through the act of observation. The observer and the observed become one, but are not one. Particles entangle with one another in such a way that they cannot be described as elements in themselves any longer but intimately reflect each other and their changes as if they are one and yet not one. Finally, a quantum can at the same time be both a wave and a particle without being either.

Postmodern science then allows us to reenvision the traditional concept of the Trinitarian mystery. While recent relational descriptions of the Trinity emphasize the three persons in communion,[17] postmodern science allows us to understand "relationality" in a much more radical sense of the oneness of God in which the Three are One. It moves us beyond an understanding of the Trinity as distinct persons relating to one another to that of a much fuzzier relationship of unity closer to the mystery of three in one and one in three.

In terms of the Trinitarian mission the postmodern concept of "relationality" adds a sense of depth to the words of Jesus' prayer "so that they may all be one: as you, Father, are in me, and I in you, that they also may be in us, that the world may believe that you sent me. And I have given them the glory which you gave me, that they may be one, as we are one; I in them and you in me, that they may be brought to perfection as one" (John 17:21-23). The implications of this for mission and salvation will be further developed in chapter 3 through the explication of the intimate relationship of *kenosis* (self-emptying love) to *theosis* (participating in the life of God) translating into a radical conversion to nonviolence and taking solidarity with the "other" to a new depth of Trinitarian oneness.

THIRD ANALOGY: TRINITY AS "DIFFERE(A)NCE"

The oneness of "relationality" helps us to recapture the ancient belief that "when God acts upon the world, it is never merely one of the Three who acts (with the other two standing by as helpers or mere observers), . . . it is always God who acts undividedly."[18] However, the mystery of the Trinity is not just about unity; it is also about the "threeness." Again, calling upon postmodern philosophy, Cunningham introduces the concept of "differe(a)nce" to bring a fresh perspective to understanding the "threeness" of the Trinity.

In describing the postmodern concept of "differe(a)nce" commentators tend to use it in two different senses highlighted by the use of the (e) or the (a). As simply as possible, difference refers to understanding meaning by way of contrast:

> What gives a term positive meaning is a contrast—a differential that is necessary to the meaning. . . . This "outside" operates as a foundation of sorts by holding concrete meaning in place and becomes a kind of metaphor.[19]

For example, we understand tall as not being short, green as not being red, and a chair as not being a table. In some forms of statistical analysis this led to the use of null hypotheses as a way of understanding reality. Modernity, with its desire to create universalizing theories made up of discrete categories, tends to foster this understanding. For example, the modern mind thinks about gender differences as falling into either one of two categories: male or female. The categories are distinct, exclusive, and their opposition is, if not negation, often at least hierarchical. This is difference with an (e).

"Differance" with an (a) introduces to the above idea the notion that negation is not only productive for defining what a thing is not, but it also accentuates remaining open to our understanding of a thing being more than it is. "Differance" carries with it the temporal idea of "deferring" or remaining open to more, rather than closing off our knowledge. "Differance" is more productive than simply difference because it allows us to see many more possibilities than just dichotomies. It "defers" a certain way of seeing a thing in order to perceive another pattern within it. For example,

> Imagine observing a quilt on the wall with patches of yellow, blue, and white. If you notice the yellow and the non-yellow, you see a pattern of concentric boxes. If you notice the blue and the non-blue you

see a checkered design. Each pattern is a play of differences, but it is a different set of differences when
yellow is differentiated from non-yellow than when
blue is differentiated from non-blue, a different set
of differences that shows us different patterns. . . . It
is a deferring of one pattern of differences in order
to see another pattern of differences.[20]

Related to our example of gender, "differance" would
lead us to perceive that male is different than female, but
that neither negates the other and that we must be open to
the possibility of more. For example, as a social construct,
there are a variety of potential and actual genders based
on how people perceive and define themselves. There
also are a number of biological "anomalies" that would
indicate that even physically there is more than just male
and female. Modernity deals with these events as "anomalies" while "differe(a)nce" potentially accepts them as real
events that should further encourage us to remain open to
there being more than the discreet, minimal categories we
use to understand the world.

"Differe(a)nce" then, to combine both "difference" and
"differance," relates to the mystery of the Trinity by helping us
understand the importance of the persons in defining each
other by being different and their reaching beyond themselves
by deferring closure. The Divine Three are of one substance,
but they are different and they "defer" to one another. By this
I mean that the relationship of one to the "other" is such that
the meaning of each is the "outside" of the "other." At the same
time, there is an opening of each to the "other" and the unity
of the whole to the "other" beyond itself with the potential of
becoming more.

The Father can be the Father only because there is a Son. The Son can only be the Son because there is the Father. The Father and Son are Father and Son only because of the Holy Spirit. There is the Holy Spirit because there is a Father and Son. The Trinity doesn't end there, though, because as Trinity it remains open to being more. This openness to "being more" (differe[a]nce) is what ushers forth creation with all of its diversity, plurality, and complexity. This "being more" is as much the Mission of God as is the loving embrace of the Trinity exhibited in its "relationality," solidarity, and unity.

Through the inner dynamics of the Trinity understood as "relationality" and "differe(a)nce" we are called to affirm both the unity and diversity that exist in God and creation. While the ordinary image of salvation is one in which God brings all of creation into God's self, that image needs to be nuanced by "differe(a)nce" and the expanding universe. The postmodern understanding of the Trinity opens to us the possibility of the incorporation of humanity and all creation into the divine life without being homogenized or contained by it, but, rather, by being a part of the unending expansion of the Trinity's life. In Cunningham's words, "In the postmodern era, such differance has reemerged as something for which human beings can rejoice and be thankful, rather than something that needs to be subordinated to an all-embracing desire for uniformity."[21] This vision includes a solidarity with the Trinity and all creation that recognizes the absolute necessity of the "other." The relevance of this understanding for postmodern culture should be obvious in terms of accepting the social and physical diversity and pluralism of our world. Furthermore, the implications of this for a Missio Dei understanding of mission as dialogue will be explained in chapter 4.

FOURTH ANALOGY:
TRINITY AS "EVENT"

In recapping then, I have described how through the analogy of scientific paradigm shifts we have come to be able to talk about God as Trinity. Secondly, using the concepts of postmodern hermeneutics and postmodern science, I have shown that the Trinity may not be as illogical or as unique a mystery as modernity led us to believe. Now, since my ultimate purpose is mission, I would like to touch upon the relationship between what is called the "immanent Trinity" and the "economic Trinity." Catherine Mowry LaCugna explains:

> The phrase "economic" Trinity refers to the three "faces" or manifestations of God's activity in the world, correlated with the names Father, Son and Holy Spirit. . . . "[I]mmanent" Trinity refers to the reciprocal relationships of Father, Son and Spirit to each other considered apart from God's activity in the world. [22]

She goes on to say that Karl Rahner posited the principle of the identity of the economic with the immanent Trinity and that this identification ensures commensurability between mission and procession.[23] She says:

> The mission of the Son, precisely to be the Son who discloses the Father, must be grounded in the intra-divine procession of the Son who is eternally begotten of the Father. "Otherwise, that which God is for us would tell us absolutely nothing about that which He is in Himself, as triune."[24]

There has to be some kind of relationship between the economic and immanent Trinity or none of what was revealed through Jesus would have any relevance. While LaCugna claims there is widespread agreement on this point of identification among both Protestants and Catholics, clearly objections have been raised especially by those who critique the more recent "communal" understandings of the Trinity.[25] They claim that, while there is a relationship, you can never limit God by claiming this identification. How then do we understand the relationship of immanent and economic Trinity?

John Caputo's use and understanding of "event" is another postmodern approach that helps us understand the relationship of immanent to economic in such a way that the ultimate "unknowability" of the immanent mystery is respected and the intimate relationship to it of the revealed economic is recognized.[26] Caputo's depiction of postmodern rhetoric says that behind every word there is an "event." The word points us to the "event" without totally possessing the "event." No word can actually capture in its totality an "event." Trinity, thus, refers to an "event" that exists behind or beyond the word "Trinity." It calls us forth to approach knowing the Trinity even though we can never develop a vocabulary that totally possesses it. It remains a mystery.

When he describes quantum mechanics Keith Ward offers a similar way of understanding "description" that is useful in protecting the ultimate unknowability of the immanent Trinity while speaking of the economic. He says,

> Furthermore, those waves are entangled in complex ways, which we can express mathematically but can hardly begin to imagine. There is a reality that mathematics represents without picturing. As to what really exists, we do not know. But our mathematical models work. "Description" has now been pressed to its furthest extent. The Quantum physicist is not

describing in the sense that a painter copies what he sees. The physicist is constructing elegant mathematical relationships, using numbers that do not correspond one-to-one with objective entities but that provide a nonpicturing model of a hidden but real world of fields and forces.[27]

In the next chapter I talk about the window into the heart of the Trinity found in the central revelation of the economic Trinity, the death and resurrection of Jesus. In doing so it is important to recognize that there is a real relationship between the economic Trinity and the immanent Trinity; between the paschal mystery of Jesus and a "death" within God and the Mission of God.

At the same time, it is important to remember Ward's remarks about "description" and Caputo's use of "event." These concepts help to protect the relevance of the economic Trinity and the ultimate unknowability of the immanent Trinity. That ultimate unknowability also functions to keep us open to there "being more" and the emphasis on discernment, contemplation, listening, and learning found in the four examples of living mission in the Mission of God described in chapter 5.

Finally, besides the actual words associated with the Trinity, postmodern "rhetoric" reminds us that the language of God-speak might not be logical.

> Marion develops a theory of non-predicative discourse as the sole discourse that might suit the God who, because beyond Being, would elude all predication. . . . Marion argues, the function of theological language would not be theoretical, philosophical, or metaphysical, but rather pragmatic, theo-logical and liturgical. Liturgical language would not

comprehend God within fixed metaphysical concepts but rather praise God through the ongoing performance of prayer.[28]

In the face of the vastness of the cosmos—with its splendor and majesty, its patterns and structures of relationships, its creativity and dynamic unpredictability, its kenotic[29] character that proceeds from the Divine in which it resides—the language that human beings use most effectively to speak of God is that of worship and praise. We are called to open our hearts in the language of liturgy and worship (including art, music, song, dance, and poetry) to participate in God's mission.

SUMMARY

This whole chapter has been dedicated to an examination of the mystery of God as Trinity. In trying to understand mission in postmodern culture it is assumed that a Missio Dei understanding of mission has so much more to offer than other understandings. In order to mine this conception, it is essential to begin with who God as Trinity is. For who God is greatly determines what God's mission is.

Postmodern culture offers tremendous tools for this mining process in the form of concepts from quantum mechanics and postmodern hermeneutics. Analogously, the principles of indeterminacy, entanglement, and the oneness of wave-particle duality all move us to appreciate and reflect on the true mystery of the oneness that exists within the Trinity and within creation. All is relational to a depth of Trinitarian oneness in which all is one without being one.

The principle of differe(a)nce on the other hand stirs us to value the diversity, plurality, and complexity within the Trinity and within creation. It includes the randomness of reality as found in the subatomic world, which rouses our sense of uncertainty and awakens our imaginations to the potential of there "being more."

Finally, the postmodern sense of rhetoric recaptures the sense of mystery that surrounds God and creation. Our words point to an "event" without possessing that event. Human language is limited even in how effectively it represents our own human experiences let alone the mystery we call God. Our words and our lives can only point to without possessing God and God's mission.

3

Death, God, and Trinitarian Mission

Death and the cross are thus central elements for Christians as we develop our understanding of God as Trinity and the mission of God in a postmodern culture.

Most Christians see Jesus of Nazareth as central to God's revelation and the salvation narrative we have constructed over centuries.[1] In that narrative, we understand the paschal, or life-through-death, mystery of the cross described in the Gospels as the central event of Jesus' life.[2] It is deemed the fullest, clearest, and most profound window we have into the heart of God as Trinity. Therefore, it is essential that we come to grips with this mystery using the lens of postmodern culture: first, in order to discover anew its significance for our understanding of God, God's mission, and our role in that mission. And also, to give us the means to articulate our understanding of this mystery in terms that make sense to those of us struggling in the middle space between belief in Christian mission and belief in God's revelatory presence in postmodern culture.

While it is commonly claimed that postmodernity is deeply skeptical of any overarching or metanarrative, one event that postmodern philosophers agree is universal to humans is the centrality of death and, more specifically, our consciousness of it. The famed postmodern philosopher Jacques Derrida[3] described the "gift of death" as a central event that is the basis for our singularity and individuality and therefore our personal responsibility and freedom.[4] He developed this further as the grounding for philosophical ethics and the foundation for the living of a truly human life. Even though he makes it clear that Christian revelation is unnecessary for him to arrive at this conclusion, Derrida dialogues with the thought of Jan Patocka[5] and uses many Judeo-Christian images to develop his thesis.

Reflecting on the story of Abraham in the book of Genesis, he says:

> It is finally in renouncing life, the life of his son that one has every reason to think is more precious than his own, that Abraham gains or wins. He risks winning; more precisely, having renounced winning, expecting neither response nor recompense, expecting nothing that can be given back to him, nothing that will come back to him, he sees that God gives back to him in the instant of absolute renunciation, the very thing that he had already, in the same instant, decided to sacrifice. It is given back to him because he renounced calculation.[6]

Even though he denies the need for revelation in order to arrive at his conclusion that renouncing life leads to gaining life, Derrida stresses along with Patocka that Christianity itself has not taken seriously its own central revelation nor the radical implications of it.[7]

I believe that institutional Christianity's shortcoming in this regard is not so much a failure of acknowledgment of the centrality of the paschal mystery. Rather, I would posit that it is a consequence of defining the cross and its revelation from the contexts of very different cultural milieus that make no sense for our postmodern culture. In an earlier age, the idea of sacrifice greatly influenced Christian understanding of the death of Jesus. This understanding presents God as a God who demands retribution. In the era of modernity, this vision of God became less and less acceptable to many Christians. Modernity, with its inherent belief in the perfectibility of humanity, saw death as almost an anomaly. Many theologians struggled to explain away the sting of Jesus' death by presenting it as an unfortunate consequence of a prophetic life.

Derrida's implicit challenge to those of us who struggle to understand our Christian faith in postmodern culture is to study more deeply the central message of the narrative we embrace. He forcefully implies that an atonement, or transactional, understanding of the cross bears no credibility in postmodern culture. Nor, however, does defining the cross away as an unfortunate consequence have any significance from the point of view of his thought. Rather, Derrida implies that the lens of postmodern culture, which sees death and our consciousness of it as the central mystery of who we are as human beings, will allow us to find in the central Christian mystery of the cross a new richness.[8]

Derrida is also answering the romantic conservative critics of postmodern culture who claim that culture to be a sea of relativism. He insists that meaning, morals, ethics, freedom, and responsibility do have a grounding in postmodern culture —the "gift of death." Meaning comes from learning to live into this mystery or, as the title of the last interview with Derrida manifests, from "Learning to Live, Finally."

My own attempt to look at the paschal mystery through the lens of postmodern culture has developed over time and can be divided into three different complementary stages.

Through those stages I have come to embrace three different understandings that I believe combine into a rich new meaning of the death of Jesus. These understandings can be labeled: (a) a God who suffers; (b) death resides within the Trinity; and (c) death-acceptance is the fulfillment of human incarnation. I believe that the combination of these understandings of the paschal mystery responds to the challenges of Derrida and Patocka that Christianity can become truly Christian and respond adequately to postmodern culture only by taking seriously its central mystery, the "gift of death." Acknowledging God's incarnation in postmodern culture brings fresh meaning to the revelation of this central mystery of our Christian narrative.

A GOD WHO SUFFERS

Like the postmodern philosophers of the latter half of the twentieth century, European theologians of the period were confronted with the experience of the Holocaust and the massive suffering and death associated with two world wars. The modern era's belief in the perfectibility of humanity and the natural tendency toward human development were devastated by these experiences. Thus, theologians were challenged to answer how one could possibly believe in God in the face of this suffering, death, and destruction.[9]

Like the European theologians of the latter half of the twentieth century, missionaries who lived in Africa in the 1980s and 1990s were confronted with massive suffering and death. The AIDS pandemic, poverty, regularly occurring famines, wars, and infant deaths from diarrhea and malaria moved Christians in general and Maryknoll expatriate missionaries specifically to try to understand anew our mission and how we could preach a God of love in that situation. At that time, I articulated what we called a mission statement: "Mission and Innocent Suffering." In it I declared that the suffering and death of Jesus could be seen as redemptive in a number of ways.

> First, for the innocent sufferers the Cross is the absolute affirmation of God's "being with" them. The Supreme "Being With" acknowledges their situation and in absolute compassion through Christ becomes one with them. In the ultimate situation of non-relationship, disempowerment and estrangement which characterizes the evil of innocent suffering and death, the Supreme "Being With" is present. Secondly, the death of Jesus is redemptive to the extent that it is an absolute prophetic condemnation of the sin that has caused the situations of the innocent sufferers. Their lives and their suffering are the result of sin, and Jesus' death is God's "No" to that sin.
>
> Thus, the Cross of Jesus is the ultimate act of self-giving in which the God "Being With" accepts the complete situation of "being without"—innocent death. Jesus through the act of self-sacrifice enters into the depths of inhumanity and non-relationship boldly affirming that even there "Being With" is present and the darkness of inhumanity epitomized by innocent death has been conquered. If even in that situation of utter alienation "Relationship" is fostering us back to relationship, then an eschatological hope arises—to be in oneness with ourselves and with God is never impossible—which gives birth to the church and the joy and celebration which are so

much a part of the lives of the innocent sufferers of Africa.[10]

As we look back at the development of that mission statement it is clear that consciously or unconsciously we were influenced by developments in theology in postmodern Europe led by such theologians as Jürgen Moltmann.[11]

Born in 1926 in Germany, he is one of the earliest theologians, writing at the same time as many of the postmodern philosophers, to describe in the cross the suffering of God and to reassert the importance of the cross for a Trinitarian understanding of God. He does this in the context of his own military service in World War II, his capture and life as a POW, the devastating experience of Auschwitz and the postmodern philosophical claims of the death of God. Moltmann says he is also developing his theology to correct theological interpretations of the modern period that he believes led to the marginalization of the Trinity and, I would add, the marginalization of our faith and our church.[12]

Moltmann's vision is one in which no suffering in the world, whether past, present, or future, is outside the embracing arms of a suffering God. In his book on the crucifixion, he writes:

> If that is taken seriously, it must also be said that like the Cross of Christ, even Auschwitz is in God. Even Auschwitz is taken up into the grief of the Father, the surrender of the Son and the power of the Spirit. . . . God in Auschwitz and Auschwitz in the crucified God—that is the basis for a real hope which both embraces and overcomes the world, and the ground for a love which is stronger than death and can sustain death.[13]

Maryknoll missionaries in Africa took this idea of "God suffering with us" from Moltmann and related it to our African context to theologize on how we could speak of a God of love in the context of an AIDS pandemic, gross numbers of infant mortality, and severe conditions of economic poverty. For postmodern culture, which is witnessing on a daily basis the global occurrences of devastation and destruction caused by natural and human agency, to speak of God as impassible as the romantic conservatives would have us do, is an anomaly.[14] How can a God of love be impassible? How can a God of love not suffer? Postmodern culture can revere a God who is intimately involved with us, who feels our pains, joys, and aspirations. A God who embraces us and all that that entails.

DEATH WITHIN THE TRINITY

Derrida's thought, however, and that of other postmodern philosophers raises a significant and legitimate objection to the particularity of innocent death as the focus for understanding the human mystery and the central mystery of the Christian narrative. For them, death is a universal experience and consciousness of it defines who we are as humans. Therefore, while a God who suffers may have some adequacy within postmodern culture, this God does not respond to this awareness of who we are as human beings. This adequacy comes from looking more deeply into who God is rather than what God does and then by extension who we, created in the image of God, are.

The Good Friday experience of God, as one who suffers and dies, leads quite naturally to the experience of death on Holy Saturday. However, we often simply see this day as "in between time" as we await the resurrection. We miss entirely the importance of this day and its mystery. But it is in fact this mystery that postmodern culture, as expressed in the thought of Derrida, is calling us to examine anew and take seriously as we strive to be authentic in what we proclaim and to live out our mission in postmodern culture.[15]

Moltmann understands Calvary as a unique, new event. He begins with the cross and sees it as a drama between God and God that gives birth to Trinitarian history and eschatological hope.[16] Reflecting on the mystery of Holy Saturday and as a corrective to Moltmann, Hans Urs von Balthasar (1905–88) sees in the death experience of Holy Saturday an icon of what already and continually exists within God per se. He takes the idea of a suffering God to a whole new level by seeing what happened on Calvary not so much as the start of economic Trinitarian history but as a reflection of what resides in God from all eternity and for all eternity. Von Balthasar sees Holy Saturday as the natural consequence of who God is: the Trinity already has death within it. He sees in the fate of Jesus a unique glimpse into God's internal process, a process of dying to self, a process of self-emptying love.[17]

The source of the universal character of death and our consciousness of it, highlighted by the postmoderns on a theological level, is now seen to reside within God. Death as the complete self-giving with no expectation of recompense, no expectation of response, and no calculation exists in the very heart of God. It generates the processions within the Trinity, gives birth to mission, and marks all of creation. Von Balthasar pushes us to see the self-emptying love of Jesus on the cross as reflective of the self-emptying love of God the Father in generating God the Son, who is consubstantially divine and eternal. God the Father does not see divinity as something to cling to. Rather, in an act of "super-kenosis" (eternal self-emptying),

God the Father begets the Son by totally giving over to the Son divinity. This holding on to nothing for Oneself then is the very essence of God. It harkens back to Derrida's interpretation of the Abraham story as one of total self-giving with no calculation and no motive of recompense.

> God is also free to do what God wills with God's nature. That is, God can surrender Godself; as Father, God can share his Godhead with the Son and as Father and Son, God can share the same Godhead with the Spirit.[18]

The mission of Jesus flows out of the procession of the Word made flesh from God the Father within the Trinity. In doing so, Jesus' mission points back to that procession and discloses the inner dynamics of the Trinity. The cross reveals who God is and by implication who we and all of creation are. The basis of mission is death, which is the total self-giving of oneself.

As Derrida emphasized, life is learning to live "Finally." It is learning to live into this mystery of death in such a way that our lives become truly authentic expressions of living for the "other" rather than for ourselves. My experience with university students is that even though they are influenced deeply by postmodern culture's disaffection with institutions and authorities, an authentic expression of living for the "other" is magnetic for them. They are more than willing to give legitimacy to anyone who they feel is authentically living out the value of "life for the other." That value is rooted in the act of dying to oneself (*kenosis*) which is ultimately rooted within the heart of God defined as "super-kenosis."

Jesus' Death as Fullest Expression of Incarnation

Derrida's challenge pushes us further, though, to take death seriously not just in terms of finding its origin within God and what that says about God and us, but about how the cross saves. What is wrong with humanity that needs to be saved or healed? As I said above concerning postmodern culture, an atonement understanding of the cross has very little chance of gaining legitimacy. How could a God of love demand recompense? On the other hand, finding the death on the cross as an embarrassing consequence flies in the face of the scriptural and traditional references to it as central to our salvation narrative.[19] This position also flies in the face of postmodern thought, which sees death and our consciousness of it as central to who we are as humans. How then does the cross save and what does this say about mission in postmodern culture?

According to William Frazier, two essential elements for understanding how the cross saves are: (a) the original mortality of the human race and its relationship to sin; and (b) the acceptance of death as full human "incarnation" seen as salvation.

Genesis 1–11: The Original Mortality of Humanity

I, like most Christians, was socialized into the understanding that originally human beings were created immortal and then, because of sin, became mortal. This understanding is based on the scriptural text Genesis 2:17: "for in the day that you eat of it you shall die." Traditionally, then, the relationship is expressed as sin leads to death. According to this perspective, humanity was originally created immortal and then, because of sin, death entered the scene.

On a closer reading of Genesis, though, mortality[20] was not excluded from the original condition of the human race.[21] First of all, in Genesis 2:7, humanity is clearly said to be created of two elements: dust and the breath of God. "Until you return to the ground from which you were taken; for you are dirt and to dirt you shall return" clearly refers to the primal state of humanity as one of mortality or perishability.[22] Second, the "to die" of Genesis 2:7 means rather to be cut off or excluded from communion with God. The man and the woman are driven out of the Garden and not killed. They are separated from God.[23] Third, the hunger for immortality is described as the context of the fall. Both the tree of knowledge and the tree of life of Genesis 3:22 are seen as pointing to what it is to be God. The serpent's temptation is that if humans eat of it they will become like God, and the prohibition in Genesis 3 concerning the tree of life is that they not become "immortal like us," implying that they are created mortal.[24]

Genesis[25] presents the hunger for immortality and humans' resistance to accept our mortality as the real source of sin. Sin does not lead to death, but rather resistance to death leads to sin. Death resistance is the sinful human condition that leads to sins. So, like the postmodern philosophers who see death and our consciousness of it as central to who we are as human beings, so Genesis and much of the Old and New Testaments witness to this same basic understanding that we are mortal beings, and the source of sins, the source of our failure to be truly human, is our failure to accept our mortality.[26] We either strive to be immortal or at least to worship ourselves as immortal. It is this resistance to death and our desire for immortality, then, that is the target of the salvation of the cross. What is wrong with humanity is that we do not want to be human; we do not want to accept our mortality. Because of that we involve ourselves in all sorts of destructive behavior that the wisdom of the world accepts as normal. These are attitudes and acts we engage in to preserve and build ourselves up at the expense of the "other."[27]

The Cross: Salvation as Incarnation

From what we have seen in Genesis, from the very beginning, humans resisted mortality. That resistance initiated and continues what the Christian narrative calls the history of sin. The resistance to death is ultimately a resistance to what it means to be fully human.

The cross then becomes the fullest expression of the incarnation. Bethlehem represents the beginning of the incarnation, but for Jesus as for us, incarnation is not complete until we reach death. But death is not simply that final expiration of breath at the end, but rather death and our consciousness of it journeys with us from the time of our birth. How we relate to that awareness throughout our lives hinders or fosters our becoming fully human. The salvific power of the cross comes from the way Jesus faces his death. John's Gospel (10:18) offers a clear expression of this, "No one takes it from me, but I lay it down on my own." Jesus' acceptance of death and human mortality with no calculation or motive of recompense breaks the bonds of that refusal to be human that leads to sin. It invites us to life in the full paschal humanity or full "incarnation."

This vision of the mystery of the cross plainly resonates with Derrida's vision of what it means to be human and what learning to live "Finally" really means. What Jesus did on Calvary reflects and grows out of his whole life and all he taught.[28] He lived a life centered on living "for-the-other" that could only come from the foundational attitude of accepting the de-centering of self that comes from the acceptance of our own mortality, fragility, and perishability.

The new paradigm of the cross that I am proposing as a response to postmodern culture and read through the lens of

God's presence in that culture is that death is central to understanding the Trinity both as economic (a God who suffers) and immanent. Second, the mystery of the cross is not just an event that happens on Calvary. It exists in the very essence of God. As such it shatters all the commonsense notions about God and about human life. Third, human life does not come from protecting oneself but from abandoning oneself, from emptying oneself. This attitude of selfless love can only come from a radical acceptance of our individual fragility and of the fragile and perishable nature of humanity and all of creation.

This mysterious life-through-death dynamic marks not only us but all of creation because it resides in the very essence of the Creator God. So the Spirit is poured out on creation and marks creation with the very same inner life of the Trinity. In destruction and annihilation new life is born. Human life evolved from the explosion of stars. The fullness of life can come only through the power of grace that nourishes the same dynamic of self-emptying love, of holding on to nothing for ourselves.

I have not mentioned resurrection in this description because I believe that Christians are very easily tempted to use the resurrection to deny the reality of death.[29] Traditionally we look at the cross through the lens of the resurrection. We say, "Yes, but then he rose from the dead so death is not really death." I am proposing here that we look at the resurrection through the lens of the cross. Holy Saturday really exists! Obviously for the life-through-death mystery to be real, there has to be some form of resurrection and new life. Looked at through the lens of death, the resurrection becomes God's affirmation that Jesus' death-accepting life is the "the Way, the Truth, and the Life."[30]

SUMMARY

In summary, the interpretation of the central mystery of the Christian narrative presented in this chapter sees the mission of Jesus lived through the cross as sacramental: it both points to a mystery and actualizes that mystery at the same time. The divine mystery to which Jesus' death points is the very life-through-death essence of the Trinity that defines the Trinity, us, and all of creation. Jesus himself fully actualizes that mystery on the cross by entering into what it means to be fully human and fully divine.

Our mission has to be understood in light of this drama or "process" that is being played out in history. To live the Christian mission is to live in the presence of the Trinitarian Mission and Mystery in history—to live in the presence of the gift of death from the Totally Other.

This gift and how we receive it defines our humanity. Its rejection is the source of the most pathological of evils in the world today. The denial of death in postmodern culture expresses itself in a variety of shapes and faces. The obvious efforts of science and medicine to combat aging are much more benign than the more subtle social, political, economic, militaristic, and cultural forms of protecting ourselves and our institutions (including religious institutions) at the expense of the human life of the other and creation itself.

The cross, in the Christian narrative, prophetically challenges this understanding. God comes to us as a human and reveals what true humanity is. Jesus by his death opened up the path for us by exemplifying this as "The Way." God puts the stamp of affirmation on it by raising his Son to new life. The whole paschal mystery is a sacrament of who God is, of who we are, and of God's Trinitarian Mission within which we live.

The God revealed by Jesus is a counterintuitive God.[31] Rather than being revealed as all powerful and almighty, the One True God revealed by Jesus is a God who suffers, a God within whom death resides; and a God who saves by opening up the path to a death-accepting life of self-emptying love. All of these insights flow out of looking at the cross through Derrida's perspective of the "gift of death" and have radical implications for how we Christians understand our mission within the Trinitarian Mission of God. These will be developed in the next chapter.

4

Our Mission:
A New Way of Being,
a New Way of Doing

It is to step forward without certainty but with faith and imagination to grasp the unfolding mystery of the Trinity in creation and history.

In postmodern culture, the commonsense notion is that the age of mission is over. In reaction to this attitude, John Paul II expressed in *Novo Millennio Inuente*[1] that there is an urgency and freshness to mission today with a renewed call to "set out into the deep." He further emphasized the urgency and freshness of mission in our day, referring to it in *Redemptoris Missio*[2] as a "new springtime." I am proposing that this urgency and freshness can be captured by a Missio Dei understanding of mission that resonates much more with the dominant postmodern culture of today than a "salvation through a single grand narrative" understanding of mission, no matter how nuanced that understanding may be by the romantic conservatives.

Under a Missio Dei understanding, that is, mission as belonging to or being of God, "to set out into the deep" is first to accept with awe the magnitude of the mystery of God as Trinity. Second, it is to step forward with the gift of uncertainty to grasp with faith and imagination the unfolding mystery of the Trinity in creation and history. And third, it is to be moved by that Trinitarian mystery into living in its presence through a new way of doing our mission.

The mystery of the Trinity of which I speak was described in the previous two chapters. Summarizing, it includes the mystery of unity and solidarity in which three can be one and one can be three, which a postmodern perspective of "relationality" helps us to understand. Second, the sense of openness to "otherness" in which who I am is partially defined by the "other" outside of myself and there is a continual "deferring" remaining always open to there being more. We must remain constantly open to the potential for becoming more. Third, the postmodern differentiation between word and the "event" behind the word helps to accentuate the distinction of economic and immanent Trinity. We realize that all human language falls short in describing and worshipping this Mystery, and no way can we ever fully possess the "event" of the Trinity. Finally, in the Christian narrative we believe that the clearest revelation of the very heart of this Trinity both immanent and economic is the cross. It provides insight into the dynamic process of God that gives birth to creation, to Jesus' mission, the Spirit's mission and our participation in that mission, of "self-emptying love."

In short, the radical shift implicit in Missio Dei moves us to see our mission, our participation in God's mission,[3] first, as a way of being that in turn leads to a totally different way of mission as something we "do." It is a dynamic dialectic relationship between being and doing. The way of being includes contemplation and imagination. The "doing" involves a completely new kind of acceptance of the "other" — the stranger, the foreigner, the believers of other beliefs — that is absolutely necessary for us to be who we are. The new way of "doing" mission challenges us to deny the commonsense notions of self-preservation, development, and security, and accept as the guiding principle of our lives the self-emptying love of God, in whose image we have been created and in whose presence we live. In this chapter, then, I further develop these notions of our mission within God's mission: contemplation, imagination, and "doing."

PARTICIPATION IN GOD'S MISSION AS A NEW WAY OF "BEING"

Contemplation

The admonition to "set out into the deep," understood first and foremost as accepting with awe the mystery of God and the unfolding presence of the Trinity's mission in creation and human history, challenges us to adopt a new way of being. It challenges us to be missionary by integrating listening through contemplation and imagination into our everyday activity.

Unfortunately, in our day contemplation is often understood either as the lifestyle of a select few, who separate themselves totally from the world, or simply as a tool for reaching some level of personal happiness, peace, or self-actualization. The contemplation to which I am referring is, rather, the sort one can easily imagine in the solitude of the African herder or the Montanan angler and the consciousness to which that solitude gives birth. Both the herder and the angler are very much in the world living their lives, but they find significant moments of solitude in pastures and streams, where they become aware of a mystery that is at once greater than themselves and yet an intimate part of themselves.

Picture an African herder who stands watching over his cattle graze. He leans gently on his walking stick listening to the birds, feeling the breeze, and hearing the rustling of the leaves. In this very mundane and apparently boring activity the herder can hardly avoid the sense of something bigger around him. If asked he may never be able to put words to it, but he lives it every day with the profound declaration that *Mungu yupo,* "God is here." Becoming aware of the presence of God in those moments of solitude allows him to proclaim this presence and be nourished by it even in the midst of suffering, disease, and death. In all my years of experience in Tanzania, in the face of some terrible tragedies, I never heard an African ask how God could allow these terrible things to happen. I only heard them declare, and not in a fatalistic way, "God is with us."

The Montanan angler stands waist deep in the stream, waiting hopefully just for a nibble. Alone, feeling the stream against her legs, seeing the rippling patterns of water, the brush along the bank and the rocks smoothed by age, the angler murmurs inaudible words, talking (to herself) or just a contented humming. She has a moment to recall her life, to place it in the context of the grandeur around her and to recognize the significance and insignificance of her place in that universe.

These are the moments of contemplation to which I am referring. They can take place on Fifth Avenue as easily as in a mountain retreat or a Buddhist monastery. Over a four-year period, I had the gift of an hour daily reverse train commute. Traveling the Hudson River from New York City to Ossining offers a reminder of God's gracious gift of creation. There is a spot where the Hudson bends a delicate elbow, then lets it drop again, revealing suddenly the river's immensity. There, sunlight reflects off the jagged, creviced walls of the Palisades. As I traveled the river, in my imagination I saw on its banks the forgotten souls of Native Americans, pioneers and early settlers, revolutionary and British troops, track layers and so many others who had passed before me. From their time to this new day, the river continues to flow and the Palisades to stand strong. Like the angler and the African herder, I was daily reminded of life's transience and God's eternal faithfulness and presence.

These are examples of the intimate relationship between awe of God to awe of creation that Dianne Bergant so forcefully described in her book, *The Earth Is the Lord's*.

> It is true that in the end Job stood in awe of God, but he could only do this because he had first stood in awe of God's creation. His awe went hand in hand with his admission of human limitation. In other words, Job acknowledged the intrinsic value of a world that was beyond his control. The same awe and respect are found again and again in the psalms. There, while the dignity of humankind is acclaimed, it is showcased amidst the even greater splendor of the cosmos.[4]

Driving to work, riding a train, or sitting in our living rooms, as well as in monasteries and mountain retreats, we can practice the awareness of the presence of God all around us and be filled with awe and wonder. As poet Denise Levertov wrote of Brother Lawrence:

> *everything faded, thinned to nothing, beside*
> *the light which bathed and warmed, the Presence*
> *your being had opened to. Where it shone,*
> *there life was, and abundantly; it touched*
> *your dullest task, and the task was easy.*
> *Joyful, absorbed,*

You "practiced the presence of God" as a musician
practices hour after hour his art:
"A stone before the carver,"
You "entered into yourself."[5]

When we talk about mission as God's mission and about ourselves as missionary, one element of that missionary vocation is a practiced awareness of living in the presence of God. I am talking about a radically new approach and a complete transformation of attitudes from those who see mission as primarily proclaiming a dogmatic truth of which they have unquestioned certainty.

This element of the call to be a missionary is primarily a call to be aware always of the presence of God in our being, in our midst, in our universe, and in "what God is revealing." This awareness requires the same practice that any developed talent demands plus God's grace. It comes when we affirm that God is with us (*Mungu yupo*, Emmanuel) and then with patience and discipline listen to a God who whispers.

As we'll see with regard to the four missionary examples in chapter 5, prayer and contemplation are considered as essential. Each has their own style, but they all clearly include within prayer the daily contemplative aspect of their vocation. They don't do it so they can feel good. They don't do it to be nourished, even though they all feel nourished by it. They all have this sense that God is with them, that God is guiding them in varied and mysterious ways, and that they absolutely need to quietly listen to that God with the gift of uncertainty, knowing that God is continually calling us to be more than what we are, to know more than what we know, and to do more than what we do.

Imagination

The awareness of living in the presence of God moves us even further "into the deep" to discern with imagination the working of God in the cosmos—the knowing. Imagination here refers to that human gift of being able to see anew God's revealing hand. In terms of science, on one hand, this involves the discovering of molecules, particles, and elements. But as the theoretical physicist Freeman Dyson explains, discovery has to be taken a step further by a much greater use of imagination. He describes this step by explaining the contribution of biologist Carl Woese, who found "the need for a new synthetic biology based on *emergent patterns of organization* [emphasis added] rather than on genes and molecules."[6] In other words, it is one thing to discover particles, elements, and molecules and quite another to discern the patterns of relationships among them.

Following that understanding, the challenge we face as missionaries in discerning the presence of God and the Trinity's mission primarily involves reading the developing patterns of relationships among elements in all fields—including the religious, ecological, economic, cultural, and political fields—within which humans reside. Within our narrative, we do this in the context of our scriptures, tradition, reason, and experience. This challenge compels us to seek moments of solitude to free our imaginations. Only then can we read those patterns as they are and not impose a false or partial order on them.

An example of this type of discernment that is relevant to the above challenge is that of Brother Luka Pacioli. Pacioli is credited with developing the double-entry system of bookkeeping. All of the elements already existed for the double-entry system: assets, liabilities, equity, expenses, and revenues. People had different ways of keeping track of these, but the Franciscan friar, who was steeped in the relationship of mathematics to art and architecture, was the one who looked most closely at the relationship of all of the elements to one another and imagined a pattern of relationships that described the organic symmetry and equilibrium of the system.

In our own postmodern time, we know how diverse this world is and how difficult it is to say that participating in mission is done one way around the world. Every particular situation raises its own patterns of complexity. Thus, think about the imagination it takes for missionaries to discern God's call and how to respond. Think of yourself moving into South Sudan, which has been ravaged by war for decades. Think about the sickness, the poverty, the trauma, and the potential for continuing violence. Consider the excitement of being newly independent with all its hopes and aspirations. These are the elements of the context that are challenging you to discern God's will and respond. As we will see in the next chapter, the imagination of two expatriate missionary sisters moved them to see in this field of violence, mistrust, and degradation God calling them to say, "Let's just carve out a small acreage of land where prayer and peace will reign and make it available to our neighbors."

Think of yourself moving to a country with a predominantly Muslim population and a very small Christian population. Most people have their faith and many are struggling to be faithful to it. They are suspicious of those who come in the name of another religion. So how would you participate in God's mission in this situation? In chapter 5, imagination is described as moving an elderly Christian expatriate missionary to shun the temptation of settling for serving the Christian community. Instead, he moved to a rural village to work as a hired hand with the hired hands so that he could live and pray with his Muslim family as a brother for twenty-two years.

Think what you would do if you had seen the savagery inflicted on your friends and neighbors by their own government. Think of villagers being slaughtered; young men being kidnapped and forced into military service; and constantly living in fear of the vengeful threat of the "death squads." People first hid and then, when they had the chance, ran to safety in a neighboring country. What would you do in that context? As we will see, imagination moved a Christian missionary Brother to understand God's call within that context and to say, "Let me go with them." Then, even more imaginatively, he could still find mission aging with them, sitting on an old plastic chair.

Finally, put yourself in the context of a country that has come to be known as the home of the "killing fields." Even family bonds have been devastated by the pernicious tactics of a regime bent on rule by fear. The skeletal remains of thousands and thousands who were killed are etched indelibly in the minds and hearts of the people. In the aftermath, what do you do? The patterns of mistrust, distrust, and a devastating epidemic moved the imagination of a group of expatriate missionaries to see the weakest of the weak and to reach out to care for them with no other motive than love.

The discernment of patterns of relationship, then, is "to set out into the deep" as stepping forward with healthy uncertainty to grasp the unfolding mystery of the Trinity in creation and history. Our knowledge of the world around us has changed dramatically and will change dramatically in the future, which should hasten us to a healthy uncertainty about our claims of knowledge and orthodoxy. For now we know, contrary to what others previously held, that our little planet is not the center of our solar system, and our galaxy is not the center of our universe, and our universe may not be a "uni"-verse at all or may have been born out of previous verses. However, the pattern of life, development, and change as a product of death, annihilation, and extinction appears as an inherent relationship in the universe that we know.

Human life was made possible not just through the explosion of stars but also through a process of extinction of other creatures less able to adapt to a changing environment. Our belief in the inner Trinitarian life of self-emptying love moves us to look at the universe, and within the universe at humanity, as marked by this same inner life that creates all. This great mystery of life through death that emanates from the Trinity itself nudges us, third, to "set out into the deep" to live a kenotic life. Imagination is the link between the contemplative "being" and the contemplative "doing" that is participating in God's mission.

PARTICIPATION IN GOD'S MISSION AS A NEW WAY OF "DOING"

In the post–Vatican II period, mission as what we do to participate in God's mission has moved through a gradual development of understanding that has led to a variety of elements being included as integral dimensions of our mission. Within my own missionary circle of Maryknoll we have come to accept basically five dimensions of mission. They are proclamation, witness, inter-religious dialogue, human development, and worship and praise. The move to a more Missio Dei understanding of mission pushes us then to think anew what these essential and integral elements of mission mean to ask if there is a new way of "doing" them because of our renewed sense of our mission within the Mission of God.

Proclamation

Romantic conservatives of the Roman Catholic Church along with many other denominations of the Christian tradition tend to understand mission as the proclamation of the "Good News" so that others might believe and, in believing, be saved.[7] Obviously, postmodern culture with its inherent acceptance of diversity, complexity, and pluralism has problems with this understanding. Besides the postmodern critique, postcolonial critiques have challenged this understanding, as previously mentioned, and found this form of Christian mission intimately allied with Western imperialism. Also, developments in cultural anthropology and sociology have raised important questions about ethnocentric judgments of beliefs, customs, and traditions, and have seen this type of Christian mission as a form of cultural imperialism. With these critiques, postmodern culture's challenge of this understanding has led to serious questions about the relationship of proclamation to conversion, and of conversion to salvation.

The radical shift implied by the understanding of Trinitarian mission active in creation is that salvation is not limited to humanity, let alone certain human beings. Salvation is working itself out in all of creation including, but not limited to, humanity. God's revelation on the cross was revelation about God's relationship to all of creation. This compels us to question the anthropocentric notions of mission, especially those that limit salvation to "saving souls." It also questions the ecclesiocentric notions of mission that place control over mission in the hands of a few church officials and measures success by growth. While I challenge these two misrepresentations of mission, I also realize that they led to a clear mandate on why you should proclaim the "Good News."[8] So in a postmodern world, with a profound suspicion of "grand narratives," why proclaim at all?

First, we proclaim because of the beauty of the Trinitarian mystery itself; no other reason is necessary. Revelation has led us to believe in a God radically different from all the notions we might have of God. Instead of a super transcendent Being whose name cannot be uttered, we see God as the *Abba* who did not cling to remote divinity but generated a "Son," who, though equal to the Father in all aspects, did not cling either to divinity or to humanity, and died. Together with the *Abba* he breathed out a Spirit of kenotic love that is equal to the other two in all aspects. This Trinitarian mystery of the fullness of life, which comes through death to self, is for all creation.

When we see a great movie, we naturally talk to others about it. Here within the Christian narrative we have an insight into the generating force of the universe. Through annihilation and extinction, new life comes forth and the universe continues to expand. On the human level, the Christian narrative's central insight is about what it means to be truly human. Our humanity is marked by mortality, and at the core of living a truly human life is an acceptance of that mortality: the gift of death. That acceptance leads to living a selfless life that is, counterintuitively, the fullness of self.

If, like me, you have ever met a person who radiates an aura of peace and authenticity, then you know that you are in the presence of someone who has truly accepted their mortality. Often it seems to be a quality of people who have suffered intensely. This is a mystery that deserves to be proclaimed on its own value. Proclamation really needs no other reason.

On the other hand the narrative also claims that death resistance is at the core of sin, evil, and humanly inflicted suffering. Proclamation then is motivated, second, by the desire to fight against these evils within the human community. So there is a call to conversion within this proclamation, and that call is to convert from the selfish, death-denying acts of self-interest and survival at any cost that mark our human life. It is a deep conversion of the heart that in no way implies a necessary, explicit adherence to a particular religious expression or institution. Rather it is a conversion to a death-accepting life that is a foundation for a clear vision of what is right and just. The judgment of what is evil and sinful is founded on this life-through-death mystery, and there is no hesitation to proclaim God's "no" to situations of human oppression and degradation generated by death-denying self-interest.

Finally, in the Christian narrative, there is a belief that proclamation will make available to some who will see in it an insight that not only changes them but also calls them to continue to proclaim it. The narrative thus gives birth to a community that bears it, and the bearing of the narrative involves not just the proclaiming of it, but also the study and further development of it along with the conversion of heart that leads to a changed life. There is then an explicit faith that gives birth to an explicit community dedicated to the narrative itself that encapsulates the core insight of life through death.

Witness

Living mission in the Trinitarian Mission includes a second dimension that has come to be called "presence" or "witness." In some recent analysis, this dimension of mission is often seen as necessitated by either political or sociocultural realities. Some countries have closed their doors to missionaries of other faiths, and other countries have banned open proselytizing while allowing missionaries to enter for other purposes. Over and above these realities, though, we are called by the mystery itself of Trinitarian life to live that mystery. This means a conversion of heart that allows me to see myself as a paschal being called to image God in my life by selfless love. Often we are called to live it in situations that can be perceived as totally perverse.

Reflecting on the AIDS pandemic in Africa, as said earlier, one could easily question the validity or even the possibility of believing in a God of love. As we move into a fourth generation of this disease, with staggering rates of infection and sudden increases in some populations, one asks, "Where is the God of love?" Looking into the skeletal face of someone who has diminished to just barely skin and bones, you would think that he or she would be the one to ask, "Where is your God of love?" But, they don't!

While experts search for vaccines and cures, none of which will help that person lying in front of you, the only thing you can really do is hold his hand, embrace her with loving care, and be there. This is mission as presence and witness. It is being there as a sacrament of the Trinity's presence, with no other task than to show God's love, which may be accepted or rejected.

We are also called to live this same mystery in situations that are not as perverse as these but no less demanding. A husband and wife giving up their own wants and desires for the sake of their children are equally dramatic in living out mission as witness and presence. As I rode a subway one day reading a book, I looked across to the other side and saw a very young child. He was extremely restless and would not sit still in his stroller. He would climb out, climb up on the bench, and crawl all over his mother. She looked exhausted and probably in her heart was crying for just one moment of a little peace and quiet. But denying that urge, she gently gave attention to that young boy. I questioned my own luxury of having space to read, to observe others, and to reflect on what was happening around me. The mother had no luxury. True parenting flows out of true humanity, which is the living out of the Trinitarian mystery of self-emptying love by being fully present to the child. This applies equally to the most ordinary situations of all our roles and professions.

Inter-religious Dialogue

The third dimension of living mission within the Trinitarian Mission is dialogue with the other, including ecumenical dialogue within the Christian community, interreligious dialogue with different faith expressions, and dialogue with the unaffiliated searchers. This has become a central concern in recent Roman Catholic history as the church struggles with its existence in other parts of the world alongside other major religious groups. In that struggle, labels have been used to describe the various positions.

These labels have changed over time, but for simplicity I address those that are specifically related to a salvation concept. First, *exclusivists* are those who are seen as demanding explicit conversion to the church (often perceived by the supporters of this position as their denomination) as the means to salvation. For them, Jesus is the only savior and the church is the only path to salvation. Second, *inclusivists* say that salvation comes through the life, death, and resurrection of Jesus but that salvation is meant for all of humanity. There may potentially be a variety of paths to gain access to that salvation won by Jesus by people who are living good lives even though they are following different religious expressions. Finally, *pluralists* propose that God reveals God's self in a variety of ways, all of which should be respected and studied if we are to understand God's full revelation.[9] A postmodern approach builds upon this last understanding, but goes even further.

For the postmodern, the Christian narrative of God as Trinity presents an openness to "otherness" as something that should be celebrated as an incarnation of the unity and differe(a)nce that is part of the inner Trinitarian life of the Divine. As stated in chapter 2, otherness is integral to the Trinity itself, and all otherness in creation flows out of that otherness within the life of God. Diversity and pluralism in this understanding are elements of reality that are to be celebrated and nourished rather than mutually condemned or simply to be negotiated.

In recalling the development of "differe(a)nce" in chapter 2, it was stated how opposition was not negation and how there is an absolute need for the other in the defining of the self. At one level this is exemplified by our own personal growth in self-consciousness as we interact with others. Through language and communication with the other we gradually grow in our own self-consciousness. At this level then we really cannot be who we are without the existence of the other. Over and above that, "differe(a)nce" moves us to say that opposition helps us to understand ourselves and others. We know better that something is green by opposing it to other colors like red, blue, or yellow. Finally, "differe(a)nce" moves us to remain open to there being more. This applies to my own self-understanding, to my understanding of our narrative, and to our understanding of the relationship of our narrative to other narratives.

Our vision, which grows out of the Trinitarian Mission, includes solidarity and community with God and all of creation, by recognizing the absolute necessity of the "other," of diversity, and of complexity. Therefore, we dialogue with the other so that we might more clearly know who we are. We dialogue with persons of other belief systems to help ourselves to better understand our faith and religion and to live it with more authenticity. We dialogue with others so that recognizing the grand diversity of us all we might more clearly appreciate and glorify that diversity and complexity which emanates from within the Trinitarian God.

This implies that Christians are invited to participate in God's mission by heralding the Trinitarian mystery of life, not by conquering or homogenizing others but by being a pilgrim people that is journeying and searching. One of the examples in chapter 5 speaks about living among Muslims and one day hearing a group of them thank God because Islam was the greatest of all religions. He thought to himself, "That's okay! I can allow them to say that. Jesus probably wasn't calling his followers to create the greatest religion. Didn't he say something like we should be the least?" We are a pilgrim people who, by our very faith in a Trinitarian God, whom we understand as the author of all creation, are moved to accept otherness and diversity both within our own community and outside of it.

If you look at one of the self-portraits of Vincent van Gogh, the closer you stand to it the more chaotic and distinct the brush strokes appear. As you pull back, though, the strokes meld into a consistent and recognizable face. Mission is about participating in the diverse and myriad brush strokes with which the Trinity paints this universe, a self-portrait of self-emptying love. The variety and multitude of brushstrokes meld into a masterpiece of the Divine while maintaining their "otherness" as brushstrokes.

Human Development

A fourth dimension of living mission in the Mission of the Trinity is the promotion of all of creation based on the life-through-death mystery. If we are to live our lives open to the influence of the Divine, then we are called to the radical conclusion that self-preservation and the law of survival and success, if made the foundation of our lives, are satanic. While clearly we have a responsibility to preserve life and not to commit personal or social suicide, self-preservation, if taken to be the ethical foundation of life, leads logically to a belief in the survival of the fittest. Unfortunately, examples of this way of being have become ever more numerous and public in a range of fields, especially in the economic field, where it has caused a near collapse of the global system.

Embracing the Trinitarian life-through-death mystery, we are called as part of our mission to question issues like national security, gross capital over-accumulation, and the preservation at any cost of social institutions, including the church. For example, is national security really grounds for causing innumerable people to lose their lives as they cross into our country seeking a better life for themselves and their children? Are multi-billionaires really so magnanimous when they offer charity while engaging in the gross over-accumulation of capital that allows them to be philanthropic? Is there any social institution that cannot be allowed to fail and must be protected at all cost?

Embracing the Trinitarian mystery, we are obliged to question many of those things that we as human beings do to protect and promote ourselves. Take for example the great missionary Paul the Apostle and the conversion of heart that faith in the Trinity brought about within him. He was a soldier. He firmly believed that the use of sacred force was acceptable, especially in the face of blasphemers who were questioning the very foundations of his faith, religion, and culture. After his transformation he offers this as the style of life fitting those who believe in the cruciform God:

> Bless those who persecute you: bless and do not curse them. Rejoice with those who rejoice, weep with those who weep. Live in harmony with one another; do not be haughty, but associate with the lowly; do not claim to be wiser than you are. Do not

repay anyone evil for evil, but take thought for what is noble in the sight of all. If it is possible, so far as it depends on you live peaceably with all. Beloved, never avenge yourselves. . . . No, "if your enemies are hungry, feed them; if they are thirsty, give them something to drink; for by doing this you will heap burning coals on their heads." Do not be overcome by evil but overcome evil with good.[10]

God's mission calls us to an asceticism based on a denial of self in favor of the "other." The acceptance of the Trinitarian life-through-death mystery, even with the caution above about social suicide, calls us to consider a radical and active pacifism as a true representation of our acceptance of the cross. We are called to open our hearts to live in mission under the influence of Trinitarian life as people of peace who have died to self.

Worship and Praise

Finally, as a fifth dimension of living mission in the Mission of the Trinity, worship and prayer are essential. This is distinct from and yet connected to contemplation, as described earlier. We have no words or concepts to express fully the great mystery of Being beyond being who is also intimately in and with being. Even paintings, music, song, poetry, and dance are limited in their ability to truly express the mystery of the Trinity. Given the vast expanse of the cosmos, with all its splendor and majesty, its patterns and structures of relationships, its creativity and dynamic unpredictability, its kenotic character coming from the Divine in which it resides, the language we human beings have to express our awe and acceptance are worship and praise.

We are called to open our hearts to participate in God's mission through the language of liturgy and worship. When mission is understood as Missio Dei, then everything is part of God's activity.[11] There is no separation of worship from mission. Worship is mission. It is not just a celebration of what we have done or hope to do, but also the act itself of giving praise and glory to God is probably the clearest and most appropriate form of proclamation of the Gospel. In the infancy narrative of Luke's Gospel, the shepherds are the first to hear the news of the birth of the Messiah. In that infancy narrative we hear that "the Shepherds went back singing praise to God for all they had heard and seen" (Luke 2:20).

No one who has lived in Africa can underestimate the importance of celebration, worship, and praise. Many people of Africa can spend all night in rituals of praise and prayer.[12] Our Eucharistic celebrations can learn from the African experience of the life, energy, and joy that are an essential part of liturgy and prayer. In worship and praise, we who bear the Christian narrative make our unconditional and unending affirmation, our "Amen," to the God of the dust, the God of the process, the Triune God who has marked all of creation with the paschal character of the Divine and the God who invites us: "Come, Follow Me."

SUMMARY

This chapter attempts to describe how our mission is to be understood within the paradigm of mission as God's Mission. I propose that this renewed understanding of Missio Dei will move us to some radical shifts in how we understand our own mission.

The first is an attitudinal shift that flows out of the gift of uncertainty. We are called to see our mission as one of searching and discovery rather than as one of propagating and proselytizing. This implies that our lives must be driven by contemplation and imagination as we seek the Trinitarian will and mission in all of creation.

A second major shift is the radical denial of our common-sense notions of self-preservation, development, and security. Over against notions of church expansion and protection of the church in society, the self-emptying love of God calls us, as a "kenotic community," to lives of prophetic authenticity in promoting the dignity, equality, and solidarity of all of humanity and all of creation. We are called to do this without consideration for the consequences of the place of the church in society.

Proclamation as a third major shift is an annunciation of God's eternal embrace of all of creation, including all of humanity. The call to conversion in this perspective is a call to convert from the selfish, death-denying acts of self-interest and survival at any cost to a heart filled with death-accepting self-emptying love. It is a deep conversion of the heart that in no way implies a necessary explicit adherence to a particular religious expression or social institution.

Fourth, our lives as church living out the call of God to care and love for all of creation are a symbol of the Trinitarian love and presence in creation. We are called to be a symbol pointing to God's love and actualizing that love by "being there" with no other task than to show God's love.

Fifth, since "otherness" is integral to the very inner life of the Trinity, diversity and pluralism in mission are elements of creation that are to be celebrated and nourished rather than condemned or simply negotiated. "Otherness" is a gift that helps to define us in terms of who we are and, even more importantly, reveals the very mystery and complexity of God.

Sixth, embracing the Trinitarian life-through-death mystery calls us to question major social, political, and economic policies. These include issues like national security, gross capital overaccumulation and preservation at any cost of any social institution, including the church. This embrace also calls us to see a radical and active pacifism as a true representation of our acceptance of the cross.

Seventh, the mystery of God and of creation moves us to an embrace of awe and wonder as we journey. We sojourn as a community marked by the gift of uncertainty that fills us with a sense of hope and faith. As we bear this narrative forward, it is with deep faith and hope that we accept that its future is in God's hands and not ours.

While this is a proposed understanding for mission in postmodern culture, I believe there are a number of examples of expatriate missionaries who are already living out this understanding. As I traveled around the world, I was struck most deeply by four examples that I found within the Maryknoll world. In the next chapter, I allow them to speak for themselves about their self-understandings as expatriate missionaries. I believe that their lives will put flesh on the thoughts expressed so far in this book. However, understand that they were chosen because they stood out from the norm.

5

Mission Lived

Each one embodies mission as a new way of being and does so with a gracious and healthy acceptance of the gift of uncertainty.

The questions about mission described in chapter 1 were confronting many missionaries. They may have been framed in different ways and emerged in different contexts but the fact is, from 1965 onward Christian mission in general and Roman Catholic mission specifically have been challenged by those general set of questions concerning its relevancy in a post–Vatican II context. From 2002 to 2008, I had the privilege of visiting Maryknoll missionaries around the world. I was moved by the lives of many of them, but in particular I was inspired by individuals who, I believed, had grappled with these questions and found new motivation for mission in a postmodern world.

In this chapter, I present four examples of Maryknoll missionaries who approach mission in ways that I believe reflect the influence of postmodern culture on what mission is and how we participate in it. Each one embodies mission as a new way of being and does so with a gracious and healthy acceptance of the gift of uncertainty. Each has moved very consciously in a new direction, responding to the forces of their own context and to a changed understanding of the relationship of the church to the world, the relationship of the church to the reign of God, and the relationship of the church to the "other."

They all demonstrate qualities developed in the previous chapters of contemplation, imagination in discerning God's will and proclaiming through presence, dialogue, a struggle for justice, and worship. I let each one express these qualities in his or her own words in this chapter. You will see that they all demonstrate qualities of being poetic and humble as they live in the presence of the Trinity. They live out their expatriate missionary vocations in the Sudan, Guatemala, Bangladesh, and Cambodia.

PRAYER AND PEACE PRESENCE IN SOUTH SUDAN
by Theresa Baldini and Madeline McHugh

Our mission in South Sudan invites us to a new way of loving, which is at the heart of mission, and opens us to discovering a new way of seeing, a new understanding of diversity.

Our prayer and peace presence in the Diocese of Torit in South Sudan began in 1986. In 1992 we had to flee the town of Torit when the Khartoum Army captured Kapoeta, about seventy-five miles west of Torit. We returned to the diocese in January 2000 to continue our Prayer and Peace Presence in Narus, South Sudan, where we have been until the present.

Our ministry is a very quiet, modest one, listening to the pain and often the fears of those around us and learning with our neighbors to not allow the fears or other remnants of the twenty-one-year-long war to control us. The two fields of grace that have blessed our presence in South Sudan are community and our relationships with our Sudanese neighbors. Just recently a Sudanese seminarian expressed this succinctly saying, "Just knowing you are here praying for us and your smile lifting us up are the graces we need to go on."

Some of our activities that flow from our prayer life include beginning an Association of Religious of the Diocese of Torit, where Sisters and Brothers meet twice annually for spiritual updating and sharing together. We usually give a monthly day of recollection in our area for diocesan personnel and others who wish to come, as well as spiritual direction, retreats, and liturgical services during Lent and Advent. Our dwelling is a place for others to come and imbibe prayer and peace, and thus become prayer and peace in their own lives.

Our mission in South Sudan invites us to a new way of loving, which is at the heart of mission, and opens us to discovering a new way of seeing, a new understanding of diversity. To paraphrase John's Gospel (5:19) we hear Jesus saying: "I contemplate, I see what my Gracious God is doing and this is what I do, this is how I am in mission." This kind of prayer opens us to deeper levels of compassion, which is the common denominator for our mission presence. We believe that contemplation is integral to the mission of Jesus. Prayer, meditation, and contemplation are of the utmost importance in our lives, deepening our own self-knowledge, freedom, integrity, and capacity to love.

Mission for us is primarily a "pass-over"[1] experience, in which we pass over into the lives of those around us, sharing their pain, difficulties, joys and hope. It is also about us becoming vulnerable, allowing others to "pass over" into our lives, which graces us with a deep mutual respect for one another and a deep sense of belonging. During the twenty-one years of war, and now as we move from a "culture of war" to a "culture of peace," the courageous poor in South Sudan have taught us a theology of life that, through solidarity and our common struggle, transcends death and makes hope an ongoing gift both given and received.

Our hope is the confidence that in some mysterious God-like way our lives, all our lives, have meaning, however futile they may sometimes seem to be. The meaning of our lives is in the awareness of God's presence and unconditional love for which we have no words except gratitude. This gratitude makes us realize we are not the sole authors of our stories.

One of the many ways we have experienced this hope and gratitude is reflected in our dear Sudanese friend Anna, a forty-year-old woman, who cooks for the Narus Diocesan Guest House. Anna is a mother of six children from seven to twenty years old. Her husband died suddenly in 2005, and, as is the custom in her tribe, her husband's brother sent word that he would take her into his home as wife number three.

Anna in desperation came to share this with us. We encouraged her to meet with the family and explain that as a Catholic she did not wish to have another husband and that she was able to support her family on the little salary she receives from cooking. It was a miracle that the family accepted Anna's request, but they also felt they needed to abide by the custom of asking Anna to leave the straw hut where she lived with her husband and family when her husband was alive. The hut and all the belongings in it, even Anna's clothes and those of her children, now belonged to the brother and his family. Anna and her children were moved and now share a room in a hut belonging to a friend.

When we heard of Anna's predicament, we told her that we had received a small gift and would be able to help her build a dwelling for herself and her three youngest children who still lived with her. Anna's three oldest children live with her mother in a refugee camp in Uganda and go to a secondary school there. Anna's new dwelling is made from mud bricks that have been baked in the sun; it has two rooms with small windows, and a dirt floor. Anna brought us to see her home. She is radiant with joy at having a home that is truly a "Castle" for her and her family!

Mission for us is a way of expanding our humanity as we deepen our capacity to give and receive love, as expressed in the following experiences:

◆ The many beautiful relationships we are experiencing among the Sudanese people, who continually teach us that there is no freedom within us or around us without forgiveness.

◆ We are daily seeing and being blessed by the face of God in the people around us: the displaced, the refugees, and the many people who have lost arms or legs because of the lethal shrapnel from the bombings. We are meeting the God who is continually healing wounds of despair and continually giving hope to the people.

◆ The people around us are teaching us to "live with enough." They teach us that there are two things that can dissipate the human spirit: wanting more of everything and not knowing the meaning of "enough."

◆ We are blessed by the people who believe that their destiny is to live in peace with their neighbors, including the fundamentalist Muslim government in the north, reflecting to us God's unconditional love and forgiveness.

◆ We also are learning through the suffering of the people that a salient part of being human is to try to see that no one suffers alone, that no pain goes unnoticed, and that no pain is without meaning.

- ◆ We are being blessed by the God who hears the cry of the poor (Exod. 6) and says to each of us in different ways, "I hear the cry of the poor and I am sending you!" God invites us to leave our comfortable space, to walk with God to unknown places, and to share meaningful relationships with those who touch our lives; in the process we discover God's love made visible in the people around us.

- ◆ God continually blesses and invites us to participate in a process of personal and communal transformation. This involves being on a journey into the Present Moment. Like the disciples on the road to Emmaus, we learn to recognize Jesus in the questions of our hearts and in the breaking of the bread of our lives, discovering a unity that includes our diversity. This implies trusting God in new ways, learning new and deeper reasons for loving and forgiving, becoming ministers of reconciliation, and learning to do this unconditionally.

- ◆ And in all of this, we are discovering that our real journey as missioners is inward, and the conversion is not someone else's but our own. It is an ongoing surrender to God's overwhelming love, which implies being open to having others love us. This is the essence of the "passover" experience for us, as it was for Jesus. The missionary journey is to our true self and our true home, the Heart of Love, where we are consciously aware of being connected to all peoples and to all of creation.

WHAT'S MISSION AFTER FIFTY YEARS?
by Marty Shea

It's what you do when you feel sick
sick to death
and wonder what to do
as the days run out
Its feeding a dying man
and facing your own dying
(for the first time)
It's eating the same food
with the same spoon
. . . and the same fear

It's just being there
with others
all the others in the crowd
as we seek to help one another
get close enough
to touch the hem of His garment.

For the last ten years or so I have lived and worked in a refugee relocation community. I was active in the negotiations by which the refugees and displaced people were able to come out of hiding and live like other Guatemalan citizens. I still have my house there with them, but over the years my mission seems to have changed from an active life of negotiating their return and relocation to one of accompanying them as they get on with their lives, their families, and their children.

All this began when the Guatemalan military turned on its own people in a genocidal war that reached its peak of violence in the 1980s. The people flooded out of the country in order to "save the children." My mission and my understanding of mission got caught up in those events, and I went with them to neighboring Mexico to live in the state of Campeche. Over the years, I have come to realize that the theme of my life and mission is the same as theirs, "to save the children."

What has seemed to be most important in all this was to be with them in their time of suffering. I have come to understand that God is a God of surprises and difficult challenges, and so while I never could have planned my mission, I could follow in faith where God led me. My mission has been to respond in justice and truth to the people's suffering; in that response we minister to one another. Mission then is about accompanying one another wherever that journey may take us, helping each other get close enough, as the Gospel story says, to touch the healing hem of Jesus' garment.

I have always sought to live in community and in a faith and praying community. I have found that community in Maryknoll and among the Guatemalan people as they persevered in the face of inhuman oppression. Together we have found communion and community. Mission then is to persevere in faith with God, who comes to us, suffers with us, and brings us new life. I confess I never knew where my mission would take me and I still don't, but I continue because of my deep belief that the mission of Him who went up to Jerusalem continues with and within us.

So that's the outward journey, which continues even now. However, there is also the inward journey that is the motor force of everything and the key to how each person responds in faith. What sustain me are prayer, the sacraments, and especially meditation in silence and stillness. Without the spiritual life of grace I would be lost. I find that the call to mission, which is a call to respond in discipleship, is about recognizing that mission is God's mission coming to life within and all around me.

So now my mission is to enter into the silence and stillness within and respond from that grace and intuition within. In that darkness I don't know where God is leading, but I don't have to know. The God of surprises calls, and the adventure is to respond in faith. So my mission is to continue that journey within and also with these good people of Guatemala, even as I get older (eighty next year), and it continues to be difficult.

One parable as I try to bring this reflection to some conclusion. There is a home for the aged here in the northeastern province of El Petén, with sixty-two men and women in the final years of their lives. I found myself going there regularly and just taking my place with them. In the beginning, it was very disconcerting, but the distance between us has diminished. I now find myself to be one of them, one with them, and that has made a great difference in my life and mission. The separation has broken down, and we are one. Surprised to find mission in an old plastic chair in a home for the aged!

MISSION AS WORKING
WITH THE HIRED HANDS
by Doug Venne[2]

Indeed, we have to search for God's will together.

When I was in the seminary I read *Seeds in the Desert* by René Voillaume and had a desire to join the Little Brothers of Jesus.[3] In 1975 when Maryknoll asked for volunteers for Bangladesh, the desire rushed back to me, and I signed up with the permission and advice of our regional superior.

I live my desired life among Muslims and Hindus. Originally, I worked in the farm fields with the hired hands for seven or eight years, which gained me credibility among the men and led them to accept me, a foreigner and a Christian, living in their village. I have been living now in a Muslim family compound for some twenty-two years, with my mission to be a brother among them following the spirituality of Charles de Foucauld. From this experience I have come to believe that while missionaries might have some idea of what we would like to do in mission, we must be invited to it by the people. We cannot just barge our way in.

My main activity in the village, and the most important thing I do, is prayer. I practice in earnest the speaking of my prayers. That is, I concentrate on whom I am praying to: Father, Jesus, Holy Spirit, Mary, etc. This makes prayer come to life for me. Even the Our Father and Hail Mary are not rote voicing but speaking to them, using those very words. I try to have my morning prayers and Mass early in the morning. In the hut where I live I get up at about 4:30 a.m. and pray for about one and a half hours. At noon, instead of lunch I take a siesta and then spend another hour before the Blessed Sacrament. In the evening, I say vespers and read. I usually say my rosary as I move around throughout the day, walking or waiting or traveling on a bus. I use the Jesus prayer at times and try to be recollected. While I am not trying to show the Bangladeshi people that I pray, I let them know that I have my times of prayer as do they.

In the seminary I saw my spiritual director monthly. This practice has been one of the important aspects of my mission life. I have followed it quite faithfully for fifty years. Along with monthly spiritual direction, I have a monthly desert day or retreat day. For more than thirty years now our Bangladesh Unit of Maryknoll missionaries has been meeting monthly. We don't see each other for almost a month so the meeting has the bonding power of making us a unit and not simply individuals doing our own thing. It has been crucial. As the years have passed, the sharing has become deeper as our trust in each other has developed. After a brief prayer, usually the rosary, we follow with input from one member on some article or event of interest and discuss it. This is followed by a sharing of our life in the last month and of some important events to come.

Sometime back I offered support to a doctor from New Zealand who works among the tribal people and the very poor of Bangladesh. He lives in a simple hut as I do, so we are somewhat akin. The doctor's staff includes Christians, Muslims, Hindus, and tribal people, many of whom have recovered from illness because of his care. Most of his staff has very little education, and he has taught them some basic medicine, as his service is based on "the poor caring for the poor." In daily prayer services he brings together the prayers of the various religious traditions of the members of his staff, which has served to knit them together. I started to give most of my funds to this doctor's work and later became his English secretary, computer correspondent, letter writer and confidant. He bounces ideas off me and I give my observations, non-medical, to him.

I also serve as spiritual guide to L'Arche in Bangladesh. (L'Arche is an international network of faith-based communities centered on people with developmental disabilities.) I have been interested in serving the mentally disabled since 1979, when I visited a L'Arche house in Kolkata, India. A spiritual guide for this community supports the staff and befriends the Core Members (that is, the disabled). Since all our Core Members are Muslim and many are nonverbal, it is mainly a matter of accompanying them.

When I reflect on what little I do in the village, I look up to God and say, "Lord, I am not much of a witness to your great love." In the village and indeed the whole area, I am the only Christian, when I remember to act like one. One of my prayers is to be an integral Christian, that is, one who works through reflection. What I have found is how broken I am. But at least that is a start. One can't fix what one does not know is broken. The people see me as a Christian and they know well my weaknesses, perhaps better than I. So perhaps I am just an unadorned introduction of a Christian to them.

One of my earliest experiences in interreligious dialogue happened when I was weeding some crops in a field that belonged to the father of the head Imam. He saw me in the squat position, weeding alone. He approached me and asked, "Are you a Jesuit?" Being an educated person, he probably had seen Jesuit missionaries in Kolkata earlier in his life.

"No," I answered, "but I am something like a Jesuit."

He quickly continued, "Are you here to convert our people?"

I had not followed the advice in the Letter of St. Peter to always be ready with an answer for your life, but the Lord Holy Spirit provided, "Our Prophet Isa [Jesus] asked us to go and help the poor, and I have chosen to do that among the poor of Bangladesh. If anyone comes closer to Allah because I have come, I will be happy." The Imam nodded his head, "I can accept that."

Also, very early on, I was privileged to work for an elderly Muslim (he was ninety years old). Somehow we were talking about the love of God for people, and I ventured the remark that God loves all those who do good. He quickly came back, "Poppycock. Allah loves all people the same." He put me in my place, as I quickly remembered how often St. Paul had said the same thing. Such an experience makes me more aware that persons of other faiths are not devoid of concepts of God similar to ours and that indeed we have to search for God's will together.

Lastly I would like again to use my landlord and Bangladeshi father, as he used to call himself, as one of the deepest examples of how God is present in all of us, even to those who may not know Jesus. One day he sent a message to me in my little hut. He wanted to see me. I knew he was very weak and in pain from a congested heart. The medicine he used was not very effective. When I arrived in the dark and gloomy room, he was covered with quilts to keep him warm. I bent over him and in a gravel voice he uttered, "I am going to die." My helpless reply was, "We all have to die someday." He continued, leaving me awestruck, "I want to ask your forgiveness for anything I have done against you." I did not know how to respond; my heart was in my throat. Having heard thousands and thousands of confessions of the Philippines where I served previously among Roman Catholics, I was now hearing the most sincere, unaffected confession in my ministry. All I could utter was, "You haven't done anything to offend me, but as you request, I forgive anything you may think you did against me." I asked God in my heart to forgive this good man. Though he did live another two years, much of the time in pain and weakness, I could only admire the man for his integrity.

Even now, because of him, the lines in my former religious education that seemed to divide religions have fallen from my heart. I believe that no one greater than Jesus has ever lived, that he was truly the Son of God, and that I want to follow him to the fullest. He is my hope, and I believe his gift of the Holy Spirit was made to all persons of good will. In some way Jesus' Spirit, this Divine Spirit dwells in all human creatures and all of creation. We need to look into each other's hearts to discover it, to witness to it, to praise God's glory.

GENTLE SERVICE TO THE POOREST
by Jim Noonan

*We need to do mission
as Jesus would do mission in the year 2012.*

I am a member of the Maryknoll mission team here in Cambodia. The team includes members from other missionary institutes as well. We all see our primary role as offering loving service to all of God's people here in Cambodia. A lot of energy and time goes into creating and sustaining this team, as we seek to respond to God's promptings not merely as individuals but as a community. Authority for this team resides in all the members of the team. We elect one person to be our public face. Our motivation for being here is faith, and we are nourished in our faith by prayer, community Eucharist, reflection on the Gospels, and private contemplative prayer.

My most important ministry right now in Cambodia is the AIDS ministry. I do this through a multifaceted program called Seedling of Hope, which I helped to create. This ministry touches almost every aspect of the afflicted person's life. This is needed because by the time an AIDS patient comes to us he or she has totally exhausted all available resources and support systems. These people are the poorest of the poor; many are absolutely desolate. So all of their needs come together to define our ministry. It includes advocacy, education, food, housing, direct medical care, and fundraising.

Advocacy is a major part of this ministry. We work with families and neighbors to prevent the rejection of the AIDS patient. We advocate with civil society to understand what AIDS is and what it is not. We produce educational materials and hold workshops with more than a thousand people each month. We advocate before the government and other social agencies on behalf of AIDS patients in order to secure better care and support for them. Networking with other agencies and NGOs is important in this work. We have long been an active part of the Cambodian Cooperation Committee, which has eighty to ninety organizations as members.

Now with the availability of antiretroviral drugs (ARV), AIDS patients have the opportunity to live longer lives. We have developed a very important program called "Bridges of Hope" that is designed to help people who are being treated successfully by ARVs. It helps them after treatment has been effective to reintegrate themselves into a productive and self-sufficient way of life.

For many years we have had more than two thousand clients being assisted by one or more of our eleven services. The total budget of Seedling of Hope alone is just over 1.5 million dollars a year. We need to raise this money. So fundraising takes up a significant part of my time.

Another part of my life is my sacramental ministry. Most of the Roman Catholics in Cambodia are ethnic Vietnamese. After the Pol Pot regime, when religion could once again be public, Maryknoll helped reestablish ministry with the Vietnamese. This started with training lay leaders and building small churches. Gradually we turned the Vietnamese apostolate over to the local church. Now I help out by celebrating Mass on Sundays in one of the Vietnamese communities.

Maryknoll also started a Saturday evening liturgy for the international community in Cambodia. Our participation with the other NGOs led us to discover a number of people who were searching for an opportunity to come together for prayer. The Saturday evening liturgy began small, but it has grown so much over time that we have had to establish a second Eucharist for the international community on Sundays, as the hall we used was no longer large enough for the whole congregation. People from all denominations and religions are welcome to participate. We respect our differences and give welcome to all who wish to join us.

Finally, my ministry includes offering individual spiritual direction to nine people. I meet each of them once a month. One of them is a Buddhist nun. I know she feels safe and understands I am not interested in converting her, but rather I am happy to accompany her on her spiritual journey in her religious tradition. This is a reflection of our approach. When I and other Maryknoll missionaries came to Cambodia, we wanted to build good relationships with people of other religious traditions. We have always tried to be as respectful as possible of the Buddhists, who are the majority religion. I have met the patriarch of Buddhism in Cambodia, and he has been helpful in our AIDS work.

Because of our ministries and our respectful relationships with others Maryknoll has become a much respected organization in Cambodia. I have heard it said here that we are like a moral anchor for many of the members of the NGO community in Cambodia.

I am deeply grateful for being a priest. To live the Gospel, as I understand it, is to respond to those who in their human and social needs cry out to be touched by God's love. Mission is about witnessing God's love for all. Jesus in his ministry responded to the sick and to the troubled souls of those who no one else had time for. The AIDS patients and the children impacted by AIDS who we serve in Cambodia through Seedling of Hope are those good folks who are falling through the cracks. For me as a disciple of Jesus, this ministry is about proclaiming God's love and promoting God's Kingdom. The values of the Kingdom of God—true human values—have to permeate all our work if we are to be socially relevant and helpful. They are the values that Jesus came to promote. At the Transfiguration St. Peter wanted to stay on the mountain, but Jesus said no. "You had a wonderful spiritual experience, but now let us go back down the mountain to serve and accompany the people."

I believe that this is not only my understanding but also that of the Roman Catholic Church since Vatican II. I went through a real conversion with Vatican II. I believe that what we are doing is a major part of the church's understanding of mission. We have had many church officials and other missionaries visit our programs, and when they see what we are doing they see it as mission. Pope Benedict in his encyclical on love says that the care of orphans and widows is as much mission as is the celebration of the sacraments and preaching.

The church is a very precious gift to me, like family—though like some families, it is dysfunctional in a number of ways. That doesn't make me love it less; in fact, if anything, it makes me love it more. One very serious and sad example of this dysfunction is the church's teaching and practice with regards to the Eucharist. It says that the Eucharist is the center of our lives and spirituality, and yet 40 to 60 percent of the Catholic population around the world cannot partake of the Eucharist on a weekly basis because there are no ministers to celebrate Eucharist. We know that in every community there are a few people, both men and women, who because of their depth of faith could be trained and then charged with presiding at the Eucharist. Our church officials refuse to acknowledge them. For me it seems to come down in large part to power and control. The people in authority do not want to give up their control.

The cruel and despotic Cambodian dictator Pol Pot wrote that "if our hearts are nourished neither by feelings nor compassion, then we can hold an unyielding position in our struggle." We have seen that this kind of teaching brought genocide to Cambodia. His ideas were totally the opposite of the true Gospel and human values that we proclaim. We missionaries of today need to live with much feeling and compassion. We need to do mission as Jesus would do mission in the year 2012. If we, our church, and all our social institutions are full of the right feelings of love and compassion, together what a different world we would make.

SUMMARY

In summary, these are four examples of Roman Catholic missionaries who I believe are living a model of mission apropos to postmodern culture. First, they are all deeply committed to the Christian narrative. That narrative, as all of them clearly present it, includes the belief that the Trinitarian mission of God (Missio Dei) is broader and more comprehensive than simple allegiance to a social institution or belief system. For all of them, God's love is for all of creation. Equally, God's wisdom can be discerned in all of creation. This discernment is seen as central to their lives and is expressed in contemplation, silence, and prayer. Their lives, moved by the gift of uncertainty, are lives of listening and learning, searching and journeying.

For all of them, though, it is not just a matter of blind acceptance of whatever the world presents to them, for all of them are deeply committed to the poor and the outcasts who suffer most from the death-denying oppression of the rich and the powerful. This informs their discernment in such a way that they can critically engage the world around them with a clear sense of what is just and right.

6

Mission and Ecclesial Existence

The fear of death and the associated fear of vulnerability and uncertainty is expressed in a very real fear of intimacy—intimacy with God and with one another.

Missio Dei theology emphasizes that mission is God's process, into which we are invited to participate. Accepting the presence of God in all cultures, we are called to examine anew this understanding through the lens of postmodern culture. Doing that has allowed us to explore in a fresh way the mystery of God as Trinity and the mission that flows from that very mystery. Part of that freshness is our appreciation of the depth of oneness that we are called to live with one another and all of creation. Another part is our relishing of the complexity, diversity, and variety that exist within creation and humanity, including the various ways that humans have attempted to relate to that ultimate source from which we all come.

Besides this unity and diversity within God that defines mission, a postmodern perspective sees in the cross of Jesus an insight into the very heart of God and a revelation about how true humanity emerges from our perspective of death in our own lives. Accepting our mortality is the foundation of the fullness of life. Only in losing our life can we gain it translates into a life lived for the "other," a life lived ultimately in a radically nonviolent fashion. This is the mission into which we are invited.

In responding to the invitation to participate in this mission, we are called to a new way of being and doing mission. Thus, Missio Dei does not exclude the church's having a mission but rather calls for a radical shift in how we live that ecclesial[1] mission and how we live in the ecclesial community that arises from that response.

As I stated earlier, one aspect of the church's mission is to be the bearer of the Christian narrative. In that narrative, seen through the lens of postmodern culture, disciples are called to be church by communally discerning the presence of God and the voice of wisdom in the contextual fields in which the community resides. With a contemplative attitude, they free their imaginations to discern new challenges emerging from the patterns of relationships that exist within those fields. The community does this with a healthy uncertainty because the Trinitarian mission is continually unfolding and, ultimately, a mystery beyond human comprehension.

Examining the lives of the Roman Catholic expatriate missionaries described in the previous chapter, it is evident that they have many common characteristics. These characteristics put flesh on the ideas I developed in chapters 2, 3, and 4. They all stress our mission to be one of listening and discerning God's mission and will; they all highlighted the mutuality of relationship and mission as accompaniment; they all recognize diversity as a value and describe in detail their own style of living in pluralistic societies; they all stress mission as witnessing to the love of God, which flows out of the kenotic love that resides in the heart of God; and they all stress the importance of community in their doing of mission.

Paramount among these characteristics is their sense of community. However, their sense of community is very different from traditional Roman Catholic notions of church and community. In their words, life in community is essential for nourishment, for discerning the presence and will of God, and ultimately as a symbol of the endpoint of creation. However, it is much more than that. While they may be living in areas of the world not necessarily dominated by postmodern culture, their communities, as pilgrim people, embody what the church might become to more adequately respond to our postmodern culture. They put flesh on the proposals of this book by their attitudes toward church as open to the "other," constantly looking out beyond the community, relishing the nurturing and challenging aspects of mutuality in mission, and finding freedom for intimacy that comes from overcoming the fear of death. They are living embodiments of postmodern "Ecclesial Existence."[2]

LIVING ECCLESIAL EXISTENCE:
OPENNESS TO THE "OTHER"

Looking at the examples of the previous chapter, we see that the communities of which the missionaries speak are never closed. While there may be a small number of core members, they remain quite open to those who do not believe in the Christian narrative and those who may have different interpretations of that narrative. In the Cambodian community, Christians of various denominations and persons of other faiths are welcome to worship and reflect with the core members of the group. In a minority situation, like that of Bangladesh, most of those who offer spiritual support are Muslims, and they form a very real part of the community life of the Christian expatriate missionary. In South Sudan, the Sisters' small compound is a haven of peace that offers comfort and tranquility for the distressed, who are welcomed as members of the community. Finally, an aging missionary finds community among the elderly, many of whom may not be active Christians or believers at all in the Christian narrative.

Earlier I remarked on the absolute need for the other in defining who we as Christians are. The openness of the communities described above is not simply about welcoming the "other" for emotional support, or living with the "other" out of necessity in some negotiated, respectful relationship. It is about actively involving the "other" in the discernment of God's will. In the examples above, the Buddhists, the Muslims, and Christians of other denominations reflect with the Roman Catholic missionaries on the mystery at the very heart of creation from the perspectives of their own narratives. The missionaries themselves talked about "a new way of understanding diversity" and searching for God's will together. They talk about being spiritual guides but never in terms of moving persons out of their own religious narrative.

This openness on the part of these expatriate missionaries is first of all related to their understanding of the Trinity and seeing diversity and the "other" as an expression of the inner life of the Trinity itself. As I expressed in chapter 2, creation in all its wonder and variety is generated from the diversity and otherness that exists in the differe(a)nce among the persons themselves within God. If God generates this diverse universe then diversity itself is something to be celebrated and nourished. All religious expressions are mirrors reflecting in a variety of ways God's presence. As such they all have a place in discerning God's will for all of creation.

The openness to the "other" is also related to the willingness of the missionaries' communities to look outside of themselves for their purpose. In other words, the community is not seen as an end in itself or something that needs to be protected. It is not love turned in on itself. Rather, it is love that encourages the community to go beyond where it is. It is a love that moves the community to cross over the borders to the "other" and walk with the "other."

LIVING ECCLESIAL EXISTENCE: LOOKING BEYOND

While all of the missionaries who share their stories in chapter 5 emphasize contemplative communal discernment, their focus is not themselves, nor is it prayer for its own sake or for themselves. They are always looking outside themselves for the challenges that give them life. The missionary who walks with the people of Cambodia gently comforting those suffering from AIDS finds in that action his reason for being there. As described in his reflection, "all of their needs come together to define our ministry."

A contemplative prayer community easily could be located in a tranquil setting, but these Sisters chose to set theirs in the heart of South Sudan when the worst of the violence there was raging. Common wisdom would consider this the worst location, but for the Sisters it was the most appropriate. Contemplation as an active embrace of the world at its worst is for them mission. They described it as a passing over into the lives of those around them and allowing their neighbors to pass over into their own lives. They emphasized that it is not just doing things for others but allowing others to do things for them, and especially to learn from others key insights into what it means to be human. Among these insights, the Sisters said, one of the most profound was learning from the people to "live with enough." They were taught that the two things that dissipate the human spirit are: wanting more of everything and not knowing the meaning of "enough." This resonates so profoundly with the kenotic notion of what it means to be truly human: that life is not about the over-accumulation of wealth, possessions, and success but about learning the meaning of "enough."

Imagine a successful Christian missionary in the Philippines making a conscious decision to move into a rural village in Bangladesh. He moved from a predominantly Christian country to a tiny village with no Christians. He found community among Muslim villagers, praying his prayers as they prayed theirs. He became a hired hand among hired hands, weeding a field. With humbleness he reached out beyond the village to serve the L'Arche movement, to help with medical services, and to create a prayer community that spans the globe. In his ministry to the L'Arche community, he found himself the spiritual guide for core members and staff. What that meant was to be there for those core members, who were predominantly Muslim, many of whom were nonverbal.

Finally, our aging missionary Brother could easily retire to a comfortable retirement setting in the United States. Instead, he serves those with whom he has walked back and forth from Guatemala to Mexico to Guatemala. He now lives with them "eating the same food with the same spoon, . . . with the same fear." He sits with them and finds mission in an "old plastic chair." He is still driven by the same impetus that led him to walk with the people in the first place: "to save the children."

However, while all of these examples accentuate what the missionaries do for the "other," none of them would ever portray mission as a one-way street. It is not just what the missionary does for the "other," but what in fact the missionary receives in the dynamic mutuality of relationship that exists. Most expatriate missionaries have come to appreciate that they receive much more than they give and have had their faith challenged and nourished by those who have received them.

LIVING ECCLESIAL EXISTENCE: MUTUALITY IN RELATIONSHIPS

As described in the chapter on the Trinity, "relationality" takes on a whole new meaning in the postmodern era. Using the analogies of postmodern science, "relationality" of elements is seen in such an intimate way that the elements actually become one without becoming one. The principle of indeterminacy, the wave-particle duality, and the principle of entanglement all hasten us to see relationship in a profoundly deep Trinitarian way. As I said in chapter 2, the concept of "relationality" moves us beyond an understanding of the Trinity as distinct persons relating to one another to that of a far fuzzier relationship of unity closer to the mystery of three-in-one and one-in-three.

The implications of this for ecclesial existence is that the traditional notions concerning expatriate missionaries as those who are "sent" and "gentes"[3] as those to whom we are "sent" are much less clear than we would like to believe. The borders that exist between us may be much fuzzier than those notions would imply. Often one has to ask who is being sent to whom.

This was exemplified in the missionaries' stories in the previous chapter. Each one, in his or her own words, talked about what each had learned from their neighbors and defined mission as a dynamic mutual experience. The elderly expatriate missionary working in the fields was confronted by the Imam and learned from him. He was reminded of insights within his own faith tradition by the Imam and gained confidence in understanding the kenotic implications for his church. He also gained insights into himself and said, "What I have found is how broken I am. But at least that is a start."

The missionary Brother lived his mission as accompaniment. But in that accompaniment he found a new aspect of mission, "to minister to one another." The accompaniment was no longer simply about him accompanying the refugees of Guatemala, but about them accompanying him in his aging. As he said, "Mission then is about accompanying one another wherever that journey may take us, helping each other get close enough, as the Gospel story says, to touch the healing hem of Jesus' garment."

The Sisters in South Sudan were most explicit about this aspect. They wrote, "In all of this, we are discovering that our real journey as missioner is inward and the conversion is not someone else's but our own. It is an ongoing surrender to God's overwhelming love, which implies being open to having others love us. This is the essence of the 'pass-over' experience for us as it was for Jesus. The missionary journey is to our true self and our true home, the Heart of Love, where we are consciously aware of being connected to all people and to all of creation."

To speak of the mutuality of mission is one thing; to live it is quite another. The constant surrender to God of ourselves that implies being open to having others love us more deeply implies a willingness to risk death of self. All those barricades we have created over the years to protect ourselves from hurt and pain become obstacles to experiencing the love of God and the love of the "other." Only by accepting our own vulnerability, fragility, and mortality can we experience the intimacy of true ecclesial existence.

LIVING ECCLESIAL EXISTENCE:
ACCEPTING INTIMACY

In chapter 3, I described how Missio Dei theology of mission leads us to rethink what it means to be in ecclesial mission. It has implications for a new way of being that includes contemplation and imagination so that we might read the will of our Trinitarian God in the hidden forces and fields of our lives. It has implications for how we proclaim, what we proclaim, and why we proclaim it. Finally, it has implications for how we relate to others and how we relate to God: how we live church.

The four examples of the previous chapter, as we said earlier, are in various ways living out the abstract ideas of chapters 2, 3, and 4, and in a way, they also put flesh on the ecclesiology proposed by Haight as described in endnote 2 of this chapter. Their example leads us to affirm that the church as community in a postmodern world needs to be open, nonrestrictive, encouraging of individuation, and always looking beyond itself. This is a rendition of community that clearly finds little resonance with the church of the romantic conservatives. But it also tends to idealize the communities described, ignoring the very real struggles of becoming sisters and brothers to one another and to the "other."

As I said earlier about the inner life of the Trinity, the suffering that exists in the very procession of one person from the other and the (kenotic) relationship of the persons to each other have dramatic implications for our lives in community. This Trinitarian dynamic leads to a much more real representation of community, including the pain of community, and reveals what keeps us from true healthy community. Life and life-in-community involve death, and the fear and resistance to death creates many aberrations and obstacles in our communal life.

Difficulties within communities are often presented as reflective of a lack of love, a lack of concern, or selfishness. These lacks are more deeply related to the fear of love or the fear of intimacy that in fact are almost one and the same as the fear of death. This insight was described by Louise Gluck in her poem "Crater Lake":

> *There was a war between good and evil.*
> *We decided to call the body good.*
>
> *That made death evil.*
> *It turned the soul*
> *against death completely.*
>
> *Like a foot soldier wanting*
> *to serve a great warrior, the soul*
> *wanted to side with the body.*
>
> *It turned against the dark,*
> *against the forms of death*
> *it recognized.*
>
> *Where does the voice come from*
> *that says suppose the war*
> *is evil, that says*
>
> *suppose the body did this to us*
> *made us afraid of love*[4]—

The fear of death and the associated fear of vulnerability and uncertainty is expressed in a very real fear of intimacy: intimacy with God and with one another. At the foundation of our fears and failures in communal life is the very real resistance to accept our own mortality and fragility and the mortality of the community. At the foundation of our fears and failures in relating to the "other" is our very real resistance to accept "the gift of death."

In terms of the Trinity and its mission, the acceptance of love is identified with the acceptance of *kenosis*. This self-emptying love defines then the community that takes up its narrative and the style of communal life. It defines the style of authority and leadership in the community, it defines the style of relationships among individuals within the community, and it defines the style of relationships with others outside of the community.

This style is founded on the contemplation and imagination of the ecclesial discernment of the presence of God and God's will in particular contexts. It is defined by the openness and authenticity of the intimacy that resides within the community. It embodies a true faith in the mystery of the Trinity that generates this beautifully diverse and complex world in which we live. And this faith moves us to "step out into the deep," relishing the gift of uncertainty and the mystery of creation, knowing that mission is God's and will never be limited to our humble attempts to understand it or to live it.

Notes

Preface

1. During the ten years prior to my election, I was employed by the University of Dar es Salaam, a government-sponsored university. Tanzanian immigration laws restricted an expatriate from having two forms of employment. Thus, my work permit was sponsored by the university and not the church.

2. Promulgated by His Holiness Pope Paul VI on December 7, 1965.

Introduction

1. This anecdotal statement is supported by the Pew Forum Religious Survey of 2008, which states, "The group that has experienced the greatest net loss by far is the Catholic Church. Overall, 31.4 percent of U.S. adults say that they were raised Catholic. Today, however, only 23.9 percent of adults identify with the Catholic Church, a net loss of 7.5 percentage points. How can this decline in the percentage of Catholics be reconciled with the findings from the General Social Surveys discussed in chapter 1 that show that roughly the same proportion of the population is Catholic today as was Catholic in the early 1970s? Part of the answer is that the Catholic Church has also attracted a good number of converts. But the main answer is immigration. The many people who have left the Catholic Church over the years have been replaced, to a great extent, by the large number of Catholic immigrants coming to the United States."

2. The Kuria are an ethnic group of agricultural-pastoralists who live on both sides of the border between Tanzania and Kenya. They are made up of about sixteen major clans and the Abairegi were the one with whom we lived and worked.

3. Pews were one of those items that he fought against in the construction of churches in Africa. He saw pews as an obstaclefor the people when they were moved to dance as an expression of prayer.

4. Pope Benedict XVI, *Verbum Domini: The Word of God in the Life and Mission of the Church* (Vatican City: Libreria Editrice Vaticana, 2010), 182.

5. Two distinct understandings of inculturation in Tanzania were reported by Laurenti Magesa in his *Anatomy of Inculturation* (Maryknoll, N.Y.: Orbis Books, 2004), 37. He uses two Swahili words to distinguish these understandings. One is *utamadunisho*, which denotes the process or act of making something that is alien part and parcel of a particular culture. *Umwilisho* literally means "embodiment" and, according to Magesa, refers to the event of God taking on the human condition or becoming like us. It is the incarnation.

6. Irving M. Zeitlin, *Ideology and the Development of Sociological Theory*, 4th ed. (Upper Saddle River, N.J.: Prentice-Hall, 1990), 45–65. I first read of this concept in Zeitlin's book as he describes the intellectual reaction against the optimism of the Enlightenment. Faced with change, conflict, and apparent disharmony, thinkers like Joseph de Bonald and Louis de Maistre were intent on showing the errors of individualism and the validity of traditional ideas and institutions. They both longed for the "good old days" when peace, harmony, and unity were believed to have reigned. Status and hierarchy were treated as essential to society, as was religious unity. They dreamed of reuniting Europe under the Roman Catholic Church as the foundation of peace and unity.

7. Ladislas Orsy, *Receiving the Council: Theological and Canonical Insights and Debates* (Collegeville, Minn.: Liturgical Press, 2009). On pages 131–32 he writes about this category: "This is the crux of this whole complicated problem. On the one hand, the official documents of the Holy See uphold—as described above—this new category with all its characteristics; on the other hand, as yet no pope, no council has infallibly approved of it. . . . It has been presented to the church universal by the Holy See; it must be received with due

obsequium, "respect." Yet as of now, we do not have a full comprehension of its place in our Tradition. It represents a new development that demands a considered response from the part of the episcopate and the community of theologians."

8. Ishvani Kendra, *Report and Documentation: Vatican: Benedict XVI Calls the Whole Church to Evangelization,* Mission Scan #101, Institute of Missiology and Communications, Pune, India, July 2011. In June 2010 Pope Benedict XVI officially announced the establishment of a new Pontifical Council for the New Evangelization. There is a desperate need for such a new evangelization in the secularized Western world. Many Catholics do not know what the Catholic Church actually teaches. Some have embraced what is often called a "cafeteria Catholicism," choosing what parts of the faith they will follow. Others profess the Creed but confine its influence to participation in the Liturgy on Sunday. This leads to what was warned of by the fathers of the Second Vatican Council as the "greatest error of our age, the separation between faith and life." The result of the rejection of the existence of objective truth has given birth to what was referred to by Pope Benedict XVI in his first homily as a "Dictatorship of Relativism." The contemporary culture has thrown off almost every remnant of Christian influence. It has embraced a "new" paganism, which is just the old paganism dressed up in the sophistry of an age that purports to be "enlightened" when it is desperately lost. The embrace of license over liberty, death over life, and the abuse of the goods of the earth over responsible stewardship, are all fueled by a counterfeit notion of freedom as a raw power over others and the delusion that "freedom" implies some feigned "right" to choose even what is wrong. The Pontifical Council for the New Evangelization is tasked with evangelizing countries where the Gospel was announced centuries ago, but where its presence in people's daily life seems to be all but lost.

9. Bishop Kevin Dowling of South Africa described this group as restorationists: "This is also a symbol of what has been happening in the church especially since Pope John Paul II became the

bishop of Rome and up till today—and that is restorationism; the carefully planned dismantling of the theology, ecclesiology, pastoral vision, indeed the 'opening of the windows' of Vatican II, in order to restore a previous, or more controllable, model of church through an increasingly centralized power structure, a structure which now controls everything in the life of the church through a network of Vatican congregations led by cardinals who ensure strict compliance with what is deemed by them to be 'orthodox.' Those who do not comply face censure and punishment, e.g., theologians who are forbidden to teach in Catholic faculties." "The Search for a Living Unity," *National Catholic Reporter*, July 23, 2010, 1, 9–10.

10. Roger Haight is a Roman Catholic Jesuit priest who taught at Regis College in Toronto when I was studying there. I found his course on historical ecclesiology to be extremely valuable. This course later became the basis for his trilogy on the church. He was at Union Theological Seminary when I did my sabbatical there and has been supportive of me throughout my career. The Vatican declared his writings highly questionable and denied him permission to teach theology. He, on the other hand, sees all of his writing to be an attempt to be a missionary in the new cultural context of the twenty-first century.

11. William Frazier is a Roman Catholic Maryknoll priest who taught at many Maryknoll educational institutions. He taught me at the B.A. and M.A. levels, and as a part of my sabbatical, I attended a two-week workshop that he presented on his thought. His thought has been so influential on my own that many of my presentations have been called "Frazier Lite" by some of my Maryknoll brothers. Postmodern culture has implicitly if not explicitly influenced Frazier's thought as he grapples with the central revelatory mystery of the death of Jesus. His interpretation of that life-through-death mystery can find its foundation in the very beginnings of postmodern philosophy.

12. This experience was most profoundly evident in the annual meeting of the Exclusively Missionary Societies of Apostolic Life (MISAL). These Societies represented churches from Africa, Asia,

Latin America, Europe, and North America. No matter where they were from, when I sat with expatriate missionaries in meetings and social gatherings like this, there was an immediate rapport different from when you were with clerics, religious, or laity who had not had an expatriate missionary experience.

1. Questioning the Legitimacy of Mission

1. Charles Taylor, *A Secular Age* (Cambridge, Mass.: The Belknap Press of Harvard University Press, 2007). Taylor describes this type of attitude as being very representative of the secular age. In the original development of the theory of secularism, it was believed that religious attitudes would eventually disappear. In reality, secularism has developed in such a way that religion has *not* disappeared, but rather it seems to have reemerged with a new vigor. However, as Taylor posits, people's attitudes toward religion and the religions of others has changed dramatically. According to him the secular age is epitomized by a new openness to the religions of others and that each person has the right to follow their religion without imposing it on others.

2. Congregation for the Doctrine of the Faith, *Dominus Iesus*, VI, #22.

3. David Schwinghamer, "Our Changing Vision in Tanzania" in *The Buffaloes*, Maryknoll Africa Region Publication, 1966. Fr. Schwinghamer describes the development of this understanding as having been led by two main thinkers, Pierre Charles and Vincent Lebbe in the period between the two World Wars. In this thought, Mission became the "mission," meaning the territories where the church had not yet been firmly planted. The major imperative of missionaries was church extension, he says.

4. To be fair, this document was not intended as a missiological treatise. Rather, as said, it was a warning to those involved in mission and inter-religious dialogue. As such, it was designed to set clear and precise points that needed to be maintained in order to protect the integrity of the Roman Catholic position. Because of this its language is not the language of theology but rather of law. See Vincent P.

Branick, "*Dominus Iesus* and the Ecumenical Dialogue with Catholics," *Journal of Ecumenical Studies* 38, no. 4 (September 1, 2001). He writes: "The logic and solid premises of *Dominus Iesus* appear clearly in the major divisions of the document, which are written as defined theses. The first three parts define a foundation in Christology. Part I asserts the thesis: "In the mystery of Jesus Christ, the incarnate Son of God the full revelation of divine truth is given" (no. 5). Parts II and III then deal with Jesus, the incarnate Word of God, as the unique mediator of salvation and the universal redeemer. Parts IV and V extend this vision of salvation to the church. The thesis is stated, "The fullness of Christ's salvific mystery belongs also to the church, inseparably united to her Lord." This church moreover is one and "subsists in . . . the Catholic Church" (no. 16). Part VI then draws the conclusions regarding the "deficient" nature of other religions and affirms "the necessity of conversion to Jesus Christ and of adherence to the church through baptism and the other sacraments in order to participate fully in communion with God" (no. 22). Throughout the declaration there appears the repeated application of Aristotle's square of logical oppositions, declaring a particular position as "contrary" or "in contradiction to" the Catholic faith.

The merit of this type of logic lies in the clarity of the conclusions. One can clearly correlate one's personal position with that of a group and thus see clearly whether or not one belongs. Organized groups need to draw boundaries. This logic also provides a rationality for the boundaries, which are rooted in basic principles. To the degree a church models itself on a pattern of a governing body, it must inevitably adopt a legislative mode of thinking. The difficulty arises when this mode of thinking flows over to a church's theological or self-reflective process.

The clearest, most painful problem with this type of logic in the Catholic Church lies in the way it inevitably leads to exclusions of people. Almost every major definition of doctrine that follows the format of a legally precise concept has led to a division in Christianity. One could counter that such an unfortunate consequence is simply the price of truth. A church unity based on a simple will-to-unity without a rootedness in truth is meaningless and useless. However, more pertinently, the matter to be clarified and bounded in ecumenical theology or other forms of theological discourse may not admit of such clarity. The theological matter at hand may be rooted in the conflict of paradoxical insights that can, at best, provide a spectrum of positions.

5. In the reaction of these church officials postmodernity is often equated with relativism. For example, Pope Benedict XVI in his "Address of his Holiness Benedict XVI to the Participants in the Ecclesial Diocesan Convention of Rome," Basilica of St. John Lateran, Monday, 6 June 2005, says: "Today, a particularly insidious obstacle to the task of educating is the massive presence in our society and culture of that relativism which, recognizing nothing as definitive, leaves as the ultimate criterion only the self with its desires. And under the semblance of freedom it becomes a prison for each one, for it separates people from one another, locking each person into his or her own 'ego.'

"With such a relativistic horizon, therefore, real education is not possible without the light of the truth; sooner or later, every person is in fact condemned to doubting in the goodness of his or her own life and the relationships of which it consists, the validity of his or her commitment to build with others something in common.

"Consequently, it is clear that not only must we seek to get the better of relativism in our work of forming people, but we are also called to counter its destructive predominance in society and culture. Hence, as well as the words of the church, the witness and public commitment of Christian families is very important, especially in order to reassert the inviolability of human life from conception until its natural end, the unique and irreplaceable value of the family founded on marriage and the need for legislative and administrative measures that support families in the task of bringing children into the world and raising them, an essential duty for our common future. I also offer you my heartfelt thanks for this commitment."

6. Fr. Arthur Wille describes the relationship of Maryknoll in the political life of Tanzania in his chapter "Maryknoll and Politics in

Tanzania," in *The Buffaloes*, Maryknoll Africa Region, 1996. Fr Wille was one of those priests who had a very close relationship to Julius Nyerere and maintains a very close relationship to the Nyerere family.

7. See Jan P. Van Bergen, *Development and Religion in Tanzania* (Madras, India: Diocesan Press, 1981). Also Judith Listowel, *The Making of Tanganyika* (London: Chatto and Windus, 1965).

8. Thomas Pakenham, *The Scramble for Africa* (New York: Avon Books, 1991), xxii. Livingstone proposed his "3 Cs" as the solution to the slave trade in Africa.

9. The "Seminar Study Year" is an example of this hopeful optimism for change. In response to Vatican II, the hierarchy in Tanzania proposed to develop a national pastoral plan. The method of developing it was to provide study papers written by selected experts that were then discussed by laity and officials. From these discussions, it was hoped that specific strategies and tactics would be developed to make the Roman Catholic Church more responsive to the Tanzanian context.

10. Sally Falk Moore, *Anthropology and Africa* (Charlottesville: University Press of Virginia, 1994). The roots of these two disciplines are grounded in the thought of August Comte, Herbert Spencer, Lewis Morgan, and Edward Tylor. Comte concentrated on the evolutionary character of Western society from one intellectual phase to another while Tylor was mainly concerned with the evolutions of culture from simple to complex and looked for the beginnings of culture by studying its survival in "primitive" cultures. Sociology followed the lead of Comte while anthropology followed Tylor in its early development. In her chapter "Changing Perspectives on a Changing Africa: The Work of Anthropology," she says that "In the nineteenth century the dominant theoretical prism through which all non-European peoples were perceived was evolutionary. Non-European societies were seen as locked in ancient traditions, as living archeological specimens, surviving relics of the dim past of the then 'modern' world. . . . These connections between anthropology and the colonial enterprise became the subject of considerable

academic invective in the 1960s and 1970s. Thus the colonial connection became a political issue among internal critics of anthropology just at the point at which such connection no longer had any practical relevance, that is, in a postcolonial reaction. Other attacks came from African academics who wanted to repossess the control of scholarship concerned with their own societies." This chapter is found in *Africa and the Disciplines*, ed. Robert Bates et al. (Chicago: University of Chicago Press, 1993).

11. *Encyclopedia of African History and Culture: The Colonial Era (1850 to 1960)*, vol. 4 states, about this period: independence for Africa brought tremendous intellectual change as well. A whole new field of academic inquiry, African studies, opened up. Historical scholarship on Africa entered an entirely new phase, one that could properly be called the beginning of major historical writing about Africa. Anthropology in Africa also underwent a fundamental transformation. In contrast to history there was already a major body of published studies, continuing along established paths of inquiry increasingly out of step with overall thinking about Africa. Thus while the classical earlier studies of African societies focused on small communities viewed as closed systems, anthropologists now had to show the interaction of local communities with the larger world. American scholars, moreover, began to enter the field in large numbers, and Africans also began to take their place in the ranks of anthropologists.

12. Ivan Illich's founding of the Center for Intercultural Documentation is just one example of the many who began questioning how Roman Catholics perceived mission and how it should be carried out. He was a Roman Catholic priest who reacted strongly against Pope John XXIII's call for North American missionaries to "modernize" the Latin American church. He is quoted as having said: "Upon the opening of our center I stated two of the purposes of our undertaking. The first was to help diminish the damage threatened by the papal order. Through our educational program for missionaries we intended to challenge them to face reality and themselves, and either refuse their assignments or—if they accepted—to be a little bit

less unprepared. Secondly, we wanted to gather sufficient influence among the decision-making bodies of mission-sponsoring agencies to dissuade them from implementing Pope John XXIII's plan" (Ivan Illich, *Celebration of Awareness: A Call for Institutional Revolution* [London: Marion Boyars, 1973], 47–48).

13. This concept developed also in Protestant missionary thought. In the World Mission Conference held in Bangkok in 1972 it was proposed that this temporary moratorium would allow local churches in Africa, Asia, and Latin America to develop their own priorities.

14. Schwinghamer, "Our Changing Vision in Tanzania," 10.

15. In Stephen Bevans and Roger Schroeder, *Constants in Context: A Theology of Mission for Today* (Maryknoll, N.Y.: Orbis Books, 2004), this period is referred to as the rebirth of mission after Vatican II (253–55). In 1975 Pope Paul issued an apostolic exhortation entitled *Evangelii Nuntiandi,* which describes the complex nature of mission. Six years later, a SEDOS-sponsored consultation concluded that mission is made up of the elements of proclamation, dialogue, inculturation, and liberation of the poor. Within this context there was a growing awareness that mission was in service to the liberating Reign of God.

16. The Pontifical Commission for Justice and Peace was established in the Roman Curia in January 1967 by Pope Paul VI. It grew out of Vatican II's desire to stimulate the Catholic community to foster progress in economically deprived areas and to establish social justice on an international scale. At the same time many dioceses around the world began initiating their own diocesan and national commissions of Justice and Peace. More recently, reference to ecological concerns is expressed by the title "justice and peace and the Integrity of Creation."

17. David Harvey, *The Condition of Postmodernity* (Oxford: Basil Blackwell, 1991), 12–14.

18. As described in Irving Zeitlin, *Ideology and the Development of Social Theory* (Engelwood, N.J.: Prentice-Hall, 1990).

19. The Roman Catholic Church's struggle with modernity led Roman authorities to label all those who attempted to find the presence of God within Modern culture as "modernist." "Modernism" was condemned as the "synthesis of all heresies" by Pius X in his encyclical *Pascendi* (1907). Among the leaders of the Catholic Movement were A. F. Loisy in France and George Tyrrell in England. Vital to the Catholic movement were the adoption of the critical approach to the Bible (which was by that time accepted by most Protestant churches) and the rejection of the intellectualism of scholastic theology.

20. Vatican II, Pastoral Constitution on the Church in the Modern World, chapter 3, no. 36.

21. Gerard Mannion, *Ecclesiology and Postmodernity: Questions for the Church in Our Time* (Collegeville, Minn.: Liturgical Press, 2007), 4.

22. Roger Haight, *Christian Community in History,* vol. 1 (New York: Continuum Press, 2004), 57.

23. D. Brian Austin, *The End of Certainty and the Beginning of Faith* (Macon, Ga.: Smyth and Helwys Publishing, 2000), 90.

24. Volume 3 of Haight, *Christian Community in History*, 244–45, explicitly lays out the problems raised for missionary activity by postmodernity as globalization, historical consciousness, and a pluralist consciousness. Globalization is forcing nations to recognize other nations and cultures in the economic and political spheres as they negotiate their own place in this interdependent globe. Historical consciousness that once was restricted primarily to intellectuals and academics has trickled down to the commonsense understanding of people in general. Universal and eternal truth has been shaken at its bedrock by the sense that particular location, time, and culture all influence what we believe at any particular moment. Finally, people on a large scale are beginning not only to expect difference but to appraise it positively.

25. Austin, *The End of Certainty and the Beginning of Faith*, vi.

26. Ibid., 149–50.

2. Rediscovering Mission in God

1. At the 1953 Mission Congress in Willingen, Germany, the dramatic changes of the 1950s and 1960s in missiology were initiated. While the term Missio Dei may not have been used, the understanding that it came to denote was prominent in this Congress. Karl Hartenstein is credited with coining the term in his report of the Congress. However, it has a much longer history that can be traced back to Augustine, who related it to the Trinity and through Martin Luther came into the twentieth century in the thought of Karl Barth. It denotes a dramatic shift from an anthropocentric (what we do in mission) understanding of mission to a theocentric one (what God does). This included a shift from an ecclesio-centric approach to a cosmo-centric one. (Tormod Engelsviken, "Missio Dei: The Understanding and Misunderstanding of a Theological Concept in European Churches and Missiology," *International Review of Mission*, October 1, 2003.) The strong Trinitarian notion of mission expressed in Vatican II's document *Ad Gentes* is at least partially based on the Protestant developments of this concept in the twentieth century according to Yves Congar (Stephen Bevans and Roger Schroeder, *Constants in Context* [Maryknoll, N.Y.: Orbis Books, 2004], 289). After Vatican II, Missio Dei faded out in some theological circles while it took a much more radical turn in other circles, almost denying the need for the church at all. While not denying the need for the church, even in its present form, it does question the control and power over mission that many church officials feel they have a right to exert. In fact the term "mission" was not used to refer to the church until the sixteenth century, when mission was applied to the sending of people to the "missions." Modern Missio Dei missiology is an attempt to bring together Trinitarian and Evangelizing mission. Especially for the romantic conservatives the Missio Dei concept of Vatican II gains only tacit acknowledgment and clearly threatens their notion of mission.

2. Decree on the Missionary Activity of the Church, *Ad Gentes*. Besides Missio Dei Protestant thought, Congar claims that the strong

Trinitarian notion of Vatican II's understanding of mission comes from St. Augustine's development of the relationship of the divine interior processions of the Trinity and the divine exterior missions. In the seventeenth century this was developed further by Cardinal Pierre de Bérulle.

3. This is not true only of mission. A theocentric approach to all theology is necessary as exemplified by Christopher Wright in *The Mission of God* (Downers Grove, Ill.: Intervarsity Academic Press, 2006). Rather than looking to the Bible for the biblical basis of mission, he calls upon us to look to the Bible as a missional phenomenon. It is the writings of those who were trying to understand and live in God's mission.

4. Bevans and Schroeder, *Constants in Context,* 293. As Bevans and Schroeder say, quoting Robert Schreiter: the unity in diversity of the Trinity will be a key for a theology of religious and cultural pluralism that is the mark of postmodern thought and civilization. Second, Trinitarian existence provides a strong theological foundation for mission as a dialogical process of giving and receiving, proclaiming and learning, speaking out prophetically and opening oneself for critique.

5. It is important to stress that these are possible analogies, and in no way are they meant to be used to prove the existence of God. Use of them as analogy assumes a faith in God.

6. A cultural field is similar to a social environment or milieu. It is like a force field that influences our behavior and thought. All cultural fields are made up of a variety of cultures and subcultures. One culture might be dominant in the field but not necessarily so. There may be two or more cultures competing for dominance, and individuals are influenced by these competing cultures based on their particular position within the field. As a culture, postmodernity is present in almost every cultural field around the world. It varies though in its dominance in any particular field.

7. Keith Ward, *The Big Questions in Science and Religion* (Philadelphia: Templeton Foundation Press, 2008).

8. Paul M. Collins, *The Trinity: A Guide for the Perplexed* (Edinburgh: T & T Clark, 2008), 52.

9. Ibid., 2.

10. The use of the word "enhancing" is to accentuate that postmodern at least in the field of the physical sciences should not be seen as a radical break with the scientific method but rather as a further development that results from that method.

11. David Cunningham, "The Trinity," in *The Cambridge Companion to Postmodern Theology,* ed. Kevin VanHoozer (Cambridge: Cambridge University Press, 2003), 186–202.

12. Gerald O'Collins in his *The Tripersonal God* (Mahwah, N.J.: Paulist Press, 1999) explains all the struggles that developed trying to understand this claim. One example was Athanasius, when he said "The Father does all things through the Word in the Holy Spirit. Thus the unity of the holy Triad is preserved."

13. D. Brian Austin, *The End of Certainty and the Beginning of Faith* (Macon, Ga.: Smyth and Helwys Publishing, 2000), 94.

14. Walter Greiner, *Quantum Mechanics: An Introduction* (New York: Springer, 2001), 29.

15. Brian Clegg, *The God Effect: Quantum Entanglement, Science's Strangest Phenomenon* (New York: St. Martin's Press, 2006), 1.

16. John Polkinghorne, ed., *The Trinity and an Entangled World: Relationality in Physical Science and Theology* (Grand Rapids: Eerdmans, 2010). On page 6 of this book Fr. Polkinghorne succinctly sums up the intrinsic nature of creation: "It is not possible to describe the world of subatomic physics atomistically! Nature is intrinsically relational."

17. Collins, *The Trinity,* 72–84.

18. Kevin J. Vanhoozer, *The Cambridge Companion to Postmodern Theology* (Cambridge: Cambridge University Press, 2003), 190.

19. Mary McClintock Fulkerson, "Feminist Theology," in ibid., 119.

20. L. Shawver, "What Postmodernism Can Do for Psychoanalysis: A Guide to the Postmodern Vision," *American Journal of Psychoanalysis* 56, no. 4 (1966): 371–94.

21. Cunningham, "The Trinity," 192.

22. Catherine Mowry LaCugna, *God for Us: The Trinity and Christian Life* (San Francisco: HarperSanFrancisco, 1991), 211.

23. These terms then refer back to previous endnotes about the theology of St. Augustine concerning the relationships of the persons within the Trinity and the activity of the Trinity in creation. Within the Trinity the Word Eternal proceeds from the Father and the Spirit proceeds from the Father through the Son. These are the processions. The missions are ad extra to the Trinity. They are God's activity in the world in the persons of the Father, Son, and Holy Spirit.

24. LaCugna, *God for Us*, 213.

25. These understandings of the Trinity see it as the model for human society that becomes a world community in which the diversity of humanity unites in oneness of community without destroying the diversity or uniqueness. Leonardo Boff is one of these theologians who looks to the community of the three persons in the Trinity as the ideal for human community. John Zizioulas is another who sees in the Trinity the sole model for understanding the relationship of communion to otherness. Over against these authors and LaCugna quoted above, Stanley Grenz claims that "the triumph of relationality has by no means been complete. A few theologians have broken ranks with the proponents of the reigning consensus. Instead of following the trend toward relationality, they have launched a search for a more appropriate perspective from which to understand the connection between the diversity and unity of God." He labels these theologians as those who are in search of the return of the immanent Trinity (Stanley Grenz, *Rediscovering the Triune God* [Minneapolis: Fortress Press, 2004]), 163.

26. See John D. Caputo and Gianni Vattimo, *After the Death of God,* ed. Jeffrey Robbin (New York: Columbia University Press, 2007).

27. Ward, *The Big Questions in Science and Religion,* 265.

28. Thomas A. Carlson, "Postmetaphysical Theology," in *The Cambridge Companion to Postmodern Theology,* ed. Kevin Van-Hoozer (Cambridge: Cambridge University Press, 2003), 72.

29. This Greek term means "emptying." It is descriptive of the life of Jesus, especially as Paul describes him in the second chapter of Paul's epistle to the Philippians. In interpreting this chapter of Philippians Michael Gorman describes what we as Christians are called to in following Jesus as "cruciformity," which is actually "theoformity." This relationship of cruciformity to theoformity in shorthand describes the next chapter.

3. Death, God, and Trinitarian Mission

1. Roger Haight, "Trinity and Religious Pluralism," *Journal of Ecumenical Studies* 44, no. 4 (Fall 2009). In this article Haight talks about the Trinity as narrative also. However, there is no doubt that he would see the presentation I am making here as too "Christocentric" to be relevant to postmodern culture and an understanding of religious pluralism. He would emphasize that Jesus reveals the way God is and the way God acts generally. "It is according to God's nature to self-manifest to and enter into dialogue with human beings. If God is to be known with any specificity, not merely as the vague object of an impulse or desire on our part, God must be revealed in particular contexts, symbols, places, events, and persons. . . . God can be and is revealed within the finite symbols of this world. . . . Therefore, other persons, other books, and other histories provide vehicles for God's 'appearing to' and thus defining a people religiously" (537).

2. The four Gospels clearly present the passion, death, and resurrection as the centerpiece of their narratives. There is a growth in emphasis on the resurrection with the historical evolution of the Gospels from Mark to the Gospel of John. For Paul there is absolutely no doubt that the central mystery of the Christian Way is the death and resurrection of Jesus.

3. Jacques Derrida was born in 1930 in Algeria, which was then French Algeria, to Jewish parents. He is often referred to in the context of poststructuralism and postmodern philosophy. He wrote more than forty books. After a long career of teaching and public speaking, he died in 2004. Allan Megill in *Prophets of Extremity* (Berkeley: University of California Press, 1985) says that "Derrida

renders explicit and obvious an attitude pervasive in modernist and especially in postmodernist art. Thus, his writings can help us come to grips with a large part of twentieth-century aesthetic consciousness" (261). I believe that this claim can be extended to include the central values of postmodern culture as described in this book. He writes in a long line of "postmodern" philosophers that stretches from Nietzsche (1840-1900) to Levinas (1906-95).

4. Jacques Derrida, *The Gift of Death* (Chicago: University of Chicago Press, 1995). In *Learning to Live Finally, the Last Interview,* Derrida poetically claimed, "So, to finally answer your question, no, I never learned-to-live. In fact not at all! Learning to live should mean learning to die, learning to take into account, so as to accept, absolute mortality. . . . I live my death in writing. It's the ultimate test: one expropriates oneself without knowing exactly who is being entrusted with what is left behind. Who is going to inherit and how? Will there even be any heirs."

5. Jan Patocka was a Czech philosopher (1907-77) who struggled with whether or not to become a Christian. Patocka wrote on the decline of technological society. Derrida says that Patocka's thesis is "that technological modernity doesn't neutralize anything; it causes a certain form of the demonic to reemerge. Of course, it does neutralize also, by encouraging indifference and boredom, but because of that—and to the same extent in fact—it allows the return of the demonic." Patocka goes on to talk about the affects of this on personal responsibility for our actions. The individualism of modernity misrepresents the unique self as a unique role rather than a person. "A persona and not a person," he says.

6. Ibid., 96-97.

7. Ibid., 6. My understanding of this is that Patocka, looking at the history of religions (but basically he is talking about Christianity), claims that religion (Christianity) has been defined by an emotional effervescent experience of the Other, which he calls demonic or orgiastic. He stresses that this demonic relationship to the Other grows out of the frightening reality of the core revelation of Christi-

anity about death, which human beings do not want to accept and do not want to reflect on.

8. David S. Cunningham, book review of *The Gift of Death* by Jacques Derrida in the *Anglican Theological Review* 80, no. 1 (1998): 127. Cunningham remarks, "When a non-Christian philosopher of great erudition pays close attention to theological questions over which Christians are manifestly divided, we should probably pay attention. . . . Derrida scales Mount Moriah, but not Golgotha. And yet this philosopher has always been better at leading theologians to see the Promised Land rather than dwelling there himself."

9. Shelly Rambo, *Spirit and Trauma: A Theology of Remaining* (Louisville: Westminster John Knox Press, 2010). She says on page 5, "In the mid- to late-twentieth century, the question of suffering—divine suffering—was at the forefront of contemporary theology. Theologian Jürgen Moltmann revolutionized Christian interpretations of the crucifixion by claiming that God did not stand outside of the event of the cross but, rather, experienced the suffering. Reformulating the concept of the Trinity and dismantling notions of divine impassibility, Moltmann provided a Christian theological response to the Holocaust."

10. In the 1990s members of the Maryknoll community in Africa began a period of communal reflection on our experience in Africa with the view of developing a vision statement that would guide our apostolate in Africa for a few years into the future. Poverty of course was a major experience, but more central at that time was the emergence of the AIDS pandemic. All of us in different ways were experiencing this massive death of humanity. In this context we then developed a document that came to be called "Mission and Innocent Suffering" (*AFER* 38, no. 5 [October 1996]: 306–17).

Summarizing it, we wrote: "From the incarnation and before until the very death of Jesus, the importance of the innocence of the sacrifice is emphasized. The animal to be slaughtered was to be one without blemish or stain. Abraham was asked to sacrifice his innocent son. At the birth of Jesus, the world was filled with the cry of the Holy Innocents. Pilate proclaimed that he could find no fault. The thief reprimanded his fellow thief saying that this person is innocent and does not deserve this suffering and death.

"At the very depth of the human mystery is the anxiety that we do not control our own destiny. While associated with death in general, it is most dramatic at those specific points when human beings suffer even to the point of death for no apparent reason or fault of their own. The Person-God Christ suffered and died as an innocent victim. Like the African sacrifice of a pure white goat who is pierced so exactly in order to extend the suffering and delay the death, so Jesus was nailed to a cross to insure the slow and agonizing death of an innocent sacrificial lamb. Throughout his journey on earth, Jesus made it absolutely clear that he had come for those who were perceived by the dominant culture and classes to be outside of relationship with the other. In every town, village, and roadside watering hole, he found the outcasts, the despised, the perceived unclean, the weak, the victims and the perceived sinners. He explicitly indicated that the universality of salvation that he had brought was directly related to the specificity of their situations of innocent suffering. The reign of God as complete oneness with one another and with God would reach its culmination only when the sin that their situation reflected was taken away."

This vision statement was presented at the 1996 Maryknoll General Chapter at which both Bill Frazier and I were present. Frazier reacted to that presentation with some clarifications, and from then on we have continued to converse. I came to appreciate more and more his thought and how radical it is. This was confirmed all the more for me when I read Derrida's critique of lived Christianity in *The Gift of Death*.

11. This probably happened more directly through many liberation theologians published by Maryknoll's Orbis Books during this period. Daniel Carroll in reviewing *A Broad Place: An Autobiography* summarizes well the influences of Moltmann on these theologians. One striking example described by Moltmann in his autobiography is found on page 196. "In 1990 I received a letter from Robert McAfee Brown. He had just come back from San Salvador and sent

this report. On November 16, 1989 government soldiers murdered with archaic brutality six Jesuit fathers in the Jesuit university UCA as well as their housekeeper and her daughter. . . . When the murderers dragged some of the bodies back into the building, they pulled the dead Román Moreno into Jon Sobrino's room. They knocked against a bookcase and a book fell on the floor and was soaked with the martyr's blood. When it was picked up next morning, it was found to be your *The Crucified God*." Carroll further describes the influence of *The Theology of Hope, The Trinity and the Kingdom of God, The Spirit of Life*, and other works.

12. In Jürgen Moltmann, *The Trinity and the Kingdom* (Minneapolis: Fortress Press, 1993), 3, he says "Assuming the presuppositions of our modern, subjective concept of experience, the transformation of dogmatics into the doctrine of faith and the conversion of the church's doctrine of the Trinity into abstract monotheism, is inescapable." He is thus affirming what I said earlier about modernity and its neutralizing affect on the belief in God as Trinity.

He himself calls for much more emphasis on what the paschal mystery of Jesus tells us about God per se. From the beginning of Trinitarian history (the cross) Moltmann looks forward to a time, the end times, when God will turn suffering into joy. As he writes, "In our experience of God we experience—fragmentarily, indeed, and certainly 'in a glass, darkly'—something of God's own experience with us. The more we understand God's experience, the more deeply the mystery of God's passion is revealed to us. We then perceive that the history of the world is the history of God's suffering. At the moments of God's profoundest revelation there is always suffering: the cry of the captives in Egypt; Jesus' cry on the cross; the sighing of the whole enslaved creation for liberty. If we once feel the infinite passion of God's love that finds expression here, then we understand the mystery of the triune God. God suffers with us—God suffers from us—God suffers for us: it is this experience of God that reveals the triune God. It has to be understood, and can only be understood in Trinitarian terms" (3–4).

13. Jürgen Moltmann, *The Crucified God* (London: SCM Press, 1989), 278.

14. Thomas Weinandy in "Does God Suffer?" (*First Things* 117 [November 2001]: 35–41, 36) asserts, "I believe that the entire project on behalf of a passible and so suffering God is utterly misconceived, philosophically and theologically. It wreaks total havoc upon the entire authentic Christian Gospel."

15. Two works that have attempted to examine the depths of meaning within the Holy Saturday experience are Alan E. Lewis's *Between Cross and Resurrection: A Theology of Holy Saturday* (Grand Rapids: Eerdmans, 2001) and Rambo's *Spirit and Trauma.*

16. Gerald O'Collins, in his *The Tripersonal God* (Mahwah, N.J.: Paulist Press, 1999), states closely Frazier's own critique of Moltmann. He says, "If one pushes matters to an extreme and argues that the paschal mystery 'constitutes' or 'creates' the Trinity, as if God somehow needed such a historical process to become Trinitarian, then—paradoxically—the divine persons cannot share in that mystery inasmuch as they are not 'present' prior to the event."

17. Anne Hunt, *What Are They Saying about the Trinity?* (Mahwah, N.J.: Paulist Press, 1998). On page 61, Hunt summarizes these theological dynamics of the theology of von Balthasar.

From this perspective, depicted so dramatically by von Balthasar, we begin to perceive that it is no accident that the revelation of the mystery of the Trinity takes place in the dynamic modality of Jesus' paschal mystery. We glimpse, as if through a dark glass but dimly, that it is intrinsically appropriate to the divine being to express itself in precisely this way. In this resides von Balthasar's profound insight, and in this consists his bracing challenge to Trinitarian theology: that the paschal movement somehow conveys, like an icon, the eternal Trinitarian relations in a paradigmatic way, which is, of its very essence, expressive of eternal Trinitarian relationality.

18. Hans Urs von Balthasar, *Theo-Drama: Theological Dramatic Theory II. Dramatis Personae: Man in God,* trans. Graham Harrison (San Francisco: Ignatius Press, 1990), 256. And elsewhere he writes: "This is because the Father's generation of the Son gives him an

equally absolute and equally free divine being; and the Son's grateful response is made, not to a Father who keeps something back for himself, but a Father who has given everything he has and is. Thus their total reciprocal self-giving is expressed and 'breathed forth' in the mutual 'We' of the Spirit, who is absolute freedom, love, and gift—selflessly so, since she is only the expression of the Father-Son unity. This is God's 'blood circulation,' the mutual exchange of blood between the Persons that, as we began by saying, is the basis for there being a 'death' in God" (Hans Urs von Balthasar, *Theo-Drama: Theological Dramatic Theory V. The Last Act* [San Francisco: Ignatius Press, 1998], 245–46).

19. William Frazier, "Some Ways for Explaining the Saving Death of Jesus," unpublished 2002 edition of Lecture Notes. In the transactional cross understanding, sin is seen as an offense against God by humanity which creates, because God is infinite, an infinite debt that requires reparation. Since the offense or debt caused by humanity is infinite, only a human who is also divine could make reparation. Thus God offers Jesus as a sacrifice who pays the price, or atones, for our sins. Scripturally this view has difficulty in that it fails to recognize the primal view of humanity of being created mortal. Also, its view of God as demanding recompense conflicts with the vision of God as all loving.

The theologians who have questioned this transactional presentation most often, especially since Vatican II, present an understanding of the cross as "consequential" or "heroic." In this understanding Jesus dies because of the way he lives. The religious and political powers of the day kill him because of his heroic stance against those powers and because of his commitment to the reign of God. He is seen as a hero who lives a prophetic life and is killed because of it.

The models covered by his paper are: Transactional Cross, Conflictual Cross, Testimonial Cross, Restoration Cross, Revelational Cross, Incarnational Cross, Pathological Cross, Consequential Cross, Collateral Cross, Moralistic Cross, Reconciliational Cross, and the Trinitarian Cross.

20. While we might find it easier to accept the mortality of the body, Frazier extends this to the mortality of the soul. Only God is immortal and as he says quoting F. J. Taylor, "Man does not possess in himself this quality of deathlessness but must, if he is to overcome the destructive power of death, receive it as the gift of God." William Frazier, "Selected Documentation on the Immortality of the Soul."

21. William Frazier has made available most of the preliminary research that he has done. His "Four Openings toward a High Pathology of Death in Genesis 1-11" summarizes those biblical scholars whom he has found supporting his thesis of the original condition of human mortality. His "Traditional Views of the Relation between Death and Sin" shows the historical development of the opposite kind of thought that sees death, including biological death, as the result of sin. This summary includes Vatican II's statement that "The Christian faith teaches that bodily death, from which man would have been immune had he not sinned, will be overcome when that wholeness, which he lost through his own fault will be given once again to him by the almighty and merciful Savior" (Pastoral Constitution on the Church in the Modern World, no. 18).

22. See Diane Bergant, *The Collegeville Pastoral Dictionary of Biblical Theology* (Collegeville, Minn.: Liturgical Press, 1996), 205–6.

23. Richard Clifford and Roland Murphy, eds., *The New Jerome Biblical Commentary* (Upper Saddle River, N.J.: Prentice-Hall, 1990), 12.

24. Bruce Vawter, *On Genesis: A New Reading* (New York: Doubleday, 1977), 88. "So reasons Yahweh in the council of the Elohim, and for this reason God banished Adam and Eve from the garden of Eden to till the ground from which they had been taken and for which they had been created in the first place."

25. This hunger for immortality is further explicated in the Tower of Babel story and in the origins of a people from Abraham. The people desired a name for themselves into the future and so departed on the project of building a tower that would reach into heaven. In ancient cultures and in some modern cultures including the cultures of sub-Saharan Africa, this desiring for a name is the

same as the desire to leave behind a legacy by which we might be remembered and so attain a form of immortality. This is carried forward in terms of the story of Abraham and Sarah, a couple without children and no hope of having children.

Frazier has criticized Derrida's interpretation of the Abraham story as reducing it to a grounding for moralism. However, while I think Derrida's primary objective was to critique philosophical ethics, in the process he does shine a light on a deeper reality that is taking place in the Abraham story, namely, through renunciation comes life. Frazier's critique of Christianity in the later period of modernity is that it has been reduced like all religions to the level of ethics and morals. In his "Christian Moralism: Inviting Invader" he writes that "a grand illusion, which has been compromising Christian life and ministry in the West for more than two hundred years, assumes that the ground level of all religion is ethical and moral." This may be the result, I would add, of the same forces that in modernity have marginalized the Trinity. Modernity finds it easier to deal with the moral imperative to "be a good person" than it does with the radical dynamics of a faith in a Triune God.

26. Romans 1:25: "They exchanged the truth of God for a lie and revered and worshipped the creature rather than the creator."

27. William Frazier, "Four Openings: Toward a High Pathology of Death in Genesis 1–11," unpublished paper, p. 9. For Frazier, the test is not just the willingness to sacrifice his son. The test includes the postponement of fulfilling the promise. Abraham and Sarah wondered for thirty-five years after having received the promise. At one point, Frazier says that the main saving act is the postponement forcing Abraham and Sarah to face their mortality. He writes: "During a journey of some thirty-five years, the patriarch and his wife walked more and more deeply into the land of the living dead. Only there and then did Yahweh secure for them the life-giving name he had promised (22:11–14). Behind each and every step of Yahweh's death-dealing way of giving the patriarch a name looms a shadow of the faithless death-resistance that energized the building of the city and the tower."

28. See Nicholas Peter Harvey, *Morals and the Meaning of Jesus: Reflections on the Hard Sayings* (Cleveland: Pilgrim Press, 1993), for a description of the radical character of the message of Jesus.

29. I have heard and read scholars who say that you can't understand the cross without looking at it from the point of view of the resurrection. In fact I would say, as I believe Frazier would say, you cannot understand the resurrection except by looking at it from the perspective of the cross.

30. Joel Green, *Body, Soul and Human Life: The Nature of Humanity in the Bible* (Grand Rapids: Baker Academic, 2008). Green has a very similar take on the resurrection. On page 169 he says, "Resurrection is not soul-flight, but the exclamation point and essential affirmation that Jesus has placed on display for all to see a life of service, even service of life-giving death, and that this life carries with it the divine imprimatur." He further says on page 180, "This reminds us again that the capacity for 'afterlife' is not a property of humanity, but is a divine gift, divinely enacted. It also underscores the reality that, in eschatological salvation, we are not rescued from the cosmos in resurrection, but transformed with it in new creation."

31. A full explication of this salvific understanding can be found in Michael J. Gorman, *Inhabiting the Cruciform God: Kenosis, Justification, and Theosis in Paul's Narrative Soteriology* (Grand Rapids: Eerdmans, 2009). In short, humanity with all of creation is called to participate in the very life of God—*Theosis*. This *theosis* as a state of oneness with God is in fact salvation or the fullness of life. Since God is cruciform this *theosis* can come about only through the grace of God nourishing our own "cruciformity," which in fact is a "theoformity." A people, characterized by communal kenotic love for the good of creation, is both the means and the goal of God's salvific activity—God's Mission. The terms "cruciformity" and "Theoformity" I believe are Gorman's creation.

4. Our Mission: A New Way of Being, a New Way of Doing

1. John Paul II, "Apostolic Letter *Novo Millennio Ineunte*" at the Close of the Great Jubilee of the Year 2000, January 2001.

2. Pope John Paul II, *"Redemptoris missio: On the Permanent Validity of the Church's Missionary Mandate."*

3. This is sometimes referred to as "evangelical mission" or "*missio ecclesiae*" in the development of Missio Dei theology. Originally in Augustine up to the 1500s, mission was exclusively used to refer to God's activity. In the 1500s, it began to be used to describe our activity in being sent by the church and to designate those areas to which we were sent. Vatican II tried to bring these two together by situating the mission of the church squarely within the Mission of God. Thus, this chapter is an attempt to describe the implications of a renewed emphasis on Missio Dei for the activity of those who believe in this mystery. Our activity under this understanding includes our way of "being" and "doing."

4. Dianne Bergant, *The Earth Is the Lord's: The Bible, Ecology and Worship* (Collegeville, Minn.: Liturgical Press, 1998), 18.

5. Denise Levertov, *The Stream and the Sapphire* (New York: New Directions Publishing, 1997), 47.

6. Freeman J. Dyson, *A Many-Colored Glass: Reflections on the Place of Life in the Universe* (Charlottesville: University Press of Virginia, 2007), 13.

7. For a time in the history of missiology, church growth movement evolved and made its home at Fuller Theological Seminary. It was mainly made up of evangelical denominations and emphasized the Great Commission of Jesus. It also openly used sociological methods to understand the target audience and determine how best to package the message to attract the "seekers."

8. These theologies support their understanding by reference to the Great Commission of Matthew's Gospel (28:16–20). Other interpretations though point to Colossians 1:23, which seems more conducive to a postmodern understanding when it says that "this is the Gospel which has been proclaimed in the whole of creation under heaven; and I, Paul, have become its minister." Again Colossians reflects a much more Missio Dei understanding in which God has proclaimed in the whole of creation and we are called to serve that proclamation.

9. Terrence Merrigan, "Jacques Dupuis and the Redefinition of Inclusivism," in *In Many and Diverse Ways: In Honor of Jacques Dupuis,* ed. Daniel Kendall and Gerald O'Collins (Maryknoll, N.Y.: Orbis Books, 2003), 60.

10. Romans 12:14–21. This is as found in Michael Gorman's *Inhabiting the Cruciform God.* Gorman has an entire chapter on Paul's conversion to nonviolence. As described, Paul saw this intimate connection between the cross and resurrection and the end of violence. Living this nonviolent life is paramount for our justification and salvation as living into the Life of God.

11. See J. G. Davies, *Worship and Mission* (New York: Association Press, 1967).

12. Titus Presler, *Transfigured Night: Mission and Culture in Zimbabwe's Vigil Movement* (Pretoria: University of South Africa Press, 1999). Pressler studied the significance of night vigils in the culture of the people of Zimbabwe. He looked at how the liberation movements had discovered the usefulness of these events in mobilizing the people to support armed struggle.

5. Mission Lived

1. Here the sisters are adapting the Old Testament image associated with the liberation of the Israelites from Egypt.

2. Sadly, Fr. Venne died shortly after writing this reflection. He chose to die in Bangladesh and his desire was to be buried in his village following the customs of the Muslim villagers. This wish was not granted as church officials once again exhibited fear concerning how it would be perceived.

3. This book describes the legacy of Charles de Foucauld, who died alone in the desert in Algeria. Some seventeen years later others followed his writings and eventually came to be a family of lay and religious "fraternities," which include such groups as: the Little Brothers of Jesus; the Little Sisters of Jesus; Jesus Caritas Priest Fraternities and Jesus Caritas Lay Fraternities, to name a few.

6. Mission and Ecclesial Existence

1. Surprisingly, some dictionaries see the terms "ecclesial" and "ecclesiastical" as having similar meanings as adjectives meaning "of or relating to a church." In more recent theological works, the terms have come to have dramatically different meanings. Ecclesiastical is usually seen as relating to the more hierarchical and institutional structures of a church. For me, ecclesial emphasizes the more communal, democratic, and equal relationship of all the members within the community. It fosters the notion that all have been given gifts, and all are called to use those gifts as a community. The use of this term then is a conscious attempt to emphasize these characteristics of church as having a primary place in any postmodern rendition of church.

2. This term is taken from the title of Roger Haight's trilogy on ecclesiology: *Christian Community in History* (New York: Continuum, 2004). Volume 3 is most significant as he proposes an ecclesiology for a postmodern world. He labels that ecclesiology a "Transdenominational Ecclesiology." In *Ecclesial Existence: Christian Community in History,* vol. 3 (New York: Continuum, 2008), he is calling for an ecclesial existence at the corporate level that sees "being-a-Christian" as shared by all Christians across their home churches. This focus, he says, finds uniformity impossible and posits that the antithesis of relativity critiqued by the romantic conservatives is not uniformity but pluralism. He writes: "By pluralism I mean differences within a common framework, a definition that is repeated in the course of the work. Pluralism refers to a situation in which differences are held together within a unifying field; it points to unity amid differences. By contrast it does not refer to pure diversity, or the existence of differences that because they are unrelated, require no mediation or negotiation" (ibid., x).

In the first two volumes of this work Haight lays the groundwork for the conclusions found in volume 3. He traces the variety of ecclesiologies that have emerged throughout the centuries concerning what is the Christian church. He sees in that variety of understandings the very real struggles of Christians to understand the mystery of their relationship to God, God's mission, and their place in the world. He also sees that variety not as a weakness but as a real reflection of our limitations to know with certainty the Divine mystery and the social historical influences on our understandings. Rather than seeing one ecclesiology as right and another as wrong, Haight proposes an ecclesiology that sees all ecclesiologies as having a home. In this ecclesiology differences are not ignored, but negotiation of differences takes place in a unifying field that can be called a "transdenominational" ecclesiology.

Haight is not proposing a federation of churches or any kind of merger. Here he is proposing an ecclesiology that is able to present in dialectical fashion the apparent contradiction of unity and diversity or sameness and difference. He is developing an ecclesiology that expresses a real common understanding of the church that acknowledges differences but doesn't allow them to be divisive of the unity shared by "being a Christian."

Some of the common elements of this ecclesiology are, first, that people participate in the church for religious reasons. It is a place that offers answers to ultimate questions. Second, most Christians who belong to the church understand that it is a historical organization that began at a certain point in time and developed over time. Third, they also believe, though, that the church rests on the initiatives of God and that the church's development is a result of God's will. Fourth, Christians hold in common the central mediating role of Jesus of Nazareth, in whom God was present and acted on behalf of all of creation. Fifth, Christians see in Scripture the primary source for understanding God's will. Sixth, the primary purpose of the church is to keep alive in history the message of Jesus, to be the bearer of the Christian narrative (ibid., 109–11).

Haight's proposed ecclesiology, while referring by his own admission to an abstraction, has significant implications for how we live church in a postmodern world. He is really talking about an attitude toward the "other." Within the church, how do we relate to other theological interpretations of the Christian message? Writing in the context of postmodern culture, Haight is implicitly nudging us to take on that culture in shaping our attitudes toward the "other." A historical consciousness will allow us to perceive how we have arrived at where we are in terms of our tremendous diverse understandings of the Christian message and all of the historical, social, and political factors that have led to this diversity. A pluralist perspective will allow us to see the diversity as various glimpses into the divine mystery that is unexplainable and can be approached only through "a glass darkly." A globalized perspective will allow us to see our differences in the light of much more dramatic differences which exist in the unifying field of our shared humanity and shared ecology.

3. Taken from the Latin title, *Ad Gentes*, of the Vatican II document Decree on the Missionary Activity of the Church. The term refers to "the nations."

4. Louise Gluck, *Averno* (New York: Farrar, Straus and Giroux, 2006), 28.

Index